WINNERS and LOSERS in a TROUBLED ECONOMY

How to engage customers online to gain competitive advantage

Martyn Perks & Richard Sedley

Winners and Losers in a Troubled Economy

How to engage customers online to gain competitive advantage

www.winners-and-losers-in-a-troubled-economy.com

First published in Great Britain in 2008 by
cScape Strategic Internet Services Ltd.
4 Pear Tree Court
Clerkenwell
London EC1R 0DS
United Kingdom
www.cscape.com

A CIPR catalogue record for this book is available from the British Library.

ISBN: 978-0-9558473-0-1

Typeset in Aachen and Thesis and Garamond.

Printed and bound in the UK by
Beacon Graphics, Units 6-7, Treadaway Technical Centre, Treadaway Hill, Loudwater, High Wycombe, Bucks HP10 9RS

WINNERS
and LOSERS in a
TROUBLED ECONOMY

How to engage customers online to gain competitive advantage

About the authors

Richard Sedley
Director, cScape Customer
Engagement Unit

Martyn Perks
Business Consultant
cScape

Richard launched the **Customer Engagement Unit** in November 2006 and has built one of the largest groups of specialist consultants available in the UK. His team creates bespoke customer engagement strategies for clients that finely balance business objectives with user needs to maximise their return on investment. Richard is the Chartered Institute of Marketing's course director for social media.

r.sedley@cscape.com
www.richard-sedley.com

Martyn's experience extends from design research to branding, information architecture and usability analysis. He has written widely for several publications, including *New Media Age*, *Netimperative*, *Blueprint*, *Guardian*'s arts blog, *Architects Journal* and *spiked*, on subjects ranging from design to technology and innovation. He is an RSA fellow and has spoken at and organised numerous events and debates on both sides of the Atlantic, including World Usability Day 2007 and several held at the London Design Museum.

m.perks@cscape.com

About cScape

cScape is an award winning digital agency that has a reputation for excellence with clients in the public sector, financial services, membership organisations and commercial businesses. An emphasis on customer engagement, and associated conversion aims, underpins cScape's integrated marketing consultancy, creative design and technical development services. cScape was founded in 1996 and is one of the most well-established design and technical consulting specialists in the UK.

About the Customer Engagement Unit

cScape's **Customer Engagement Unit** (**CEU**) is made up of an elite group of specialists who each have core skills in social media, marketing, findability, analytics, virtual worlds and persuasive design. They are entirely focused on delivering improved returns against business objectives and plan, design and deliver compelling, profitable online experiences to clients.

The drawing together of leading experts in 2006 led to the creation of the *Annual Online Customer Engagement Survey* which was developed:

- to gauge awareness of customer engagement;
- to investigate the extent to which organisations prioritise it;
- to look into the barriers and opportunities for creating optimal customer experiences

In November 2007 the team decided to write *'Winners and Losers in a Troubled Economy'* in response to widespread concerns about the impact of a slow-down in the economy.

Acknowledgements

The authors would like to acknowledge the significant contribution made by our colleagues at cScape. In particular: Suzy Dean, James Heartfield, Theresa Clifford, Rob Killick, Lucy Conlan, Para Mullan, Edward Lloyd-Williams, Theo Papadakis, Sarah Woodbridge, Tim Black, Nathalie Rothschild, Marc Sibley, Marek Kornaga, Damian Michalowski and Joe Dearsley. Our thanks and appreciation also go to all our invited contributors and those who have let us reproduce their illustrations.

Please contact Theresa Clifford at t.clifford@cscape.com for more information on this publication, our services or the authors. Visit us at www.cscape.com and sign up for our quarterly newsletter with acute intelligence.

Contents

Introduction   **9**

Chapter 1   **New marketing: the old ways will not do**   **13**

Chapter 2   **The changing face of the customer**   **17**

Chapter 3   **Creating an online customer engagement strategy**   **27**

Chapter 4   **How to create your own online customer engagement successes**   **35**

Chapter 5   **The tactics for creating a customer engagement strategy**   **41**

Chapter 6   **Measuring online customer engagement**   **57**

Chapter 7   **What role can digital media play during a recession?**   **61**

Conclusion   **71**

2008 Annual Online Customer Engagement Survey highlights   74

Useful Resources   76

Endnotes   78

Index   80

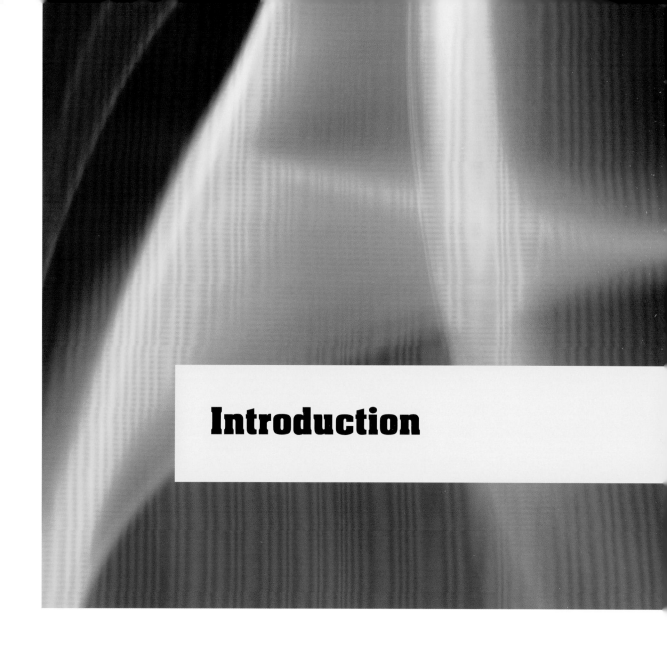

Introduction

Introduction

Are you ready for an economic downturn? If the economy hits the fan will you be able to keep your customers? Will your business survive?

If there is one thing that every previous economic slowdown, downturn, recession or slump has proved, it is that there will be winners and losers.

The focus of this publication is on how digital media, if used correctly, can create engaging customer relationships that will not only help your business now will but position you for greater success in times of plenty.

The threat of economic instability and even recession, the like of which has not been experienced for many years, poses some very serious questions. Do we carry on as before with unchanged business practices? Do we tighten our belts? Do we try to reach out to new markets and customers, recognising that the best form of defence is attack? The reality of course is that we are likely to want to do a bit of each—indeed, in many cases, we will have to. But how do we decide which, when and how?

It is our contention that by embracing customer engagement and adopting the use of digital media as the spine of your customer interactions, no matter what market you are in, you stand a far better chance of not just emerging from a downturn unscathed, but of emerging as a winner.

This book looks at what is required for creating customer engagement. It explains the value that an engaged relationship can offer and highlights some of the critical customer needs that have to be met in order to establish engagement. It defines some of the elements that will help you identify engagement, and disengagement, within your customer base and takes you through key elements of the strategy, planning and tactics required for establishing the sort of practices necessary to emerge from any economic downturn with a stronger, healthier and more engaged customer base.

It is our hope that these ideas will help shape the debate around the economy's potential impact on business and digital media. Digital more than any other channel has the capacity to engage customers in ways that can deliver value and meaning. With the threat of economic instability hanging over us, our ability to achieve high levels of customer engagement has become even more pressing.

Theses on digital customer engagement in a troubled economy

Six major theses that marketing and business professionals must consider in the years ahead.

1   **Cutting back during a downturn is a survival tactic not a winning strategy:**
Start by asking not what your customer can do for you, but what you can do for your customer.

2   **Developing customer engagement is a retention and acquisition strategy:**
Customers have practical and emotional needs—both should be met to achieve long-standing engagement.

3   **Digital media provide the best means for achieving customer engagement during a downturn:**
Dialogue, not monologue is the true language of online business.

4   **Customer engagement is the best predictor of future success:**
Customer engagement is a relationship built on mutual benefit.

5   **Responses to economic downturns are not pre-determined:**
Research and test before you assume that customers will spend less online.

6   **An economic downturn will create winners and losers:**
The winners will be those businesses that best use digital media and best engage their customers.

Customer Engagement

Repeated interactions that strengthen the emotional, psychological and physical investment a customer has in a brand (product or company).[1]

CHAPTER 1
New marketing: the old ways will not do

New marketing: the old ways will not do

When the economy is in danger of slowing down, marketing budgets are among the first to be cut. Over the coming year, marketers will be tested and their ideas will be put under the microscope. Questions will be asked as to how their budgets will return any real value. Instinctively, businesses will ration what they do. However, in times of economic slow-down businesses need to invest more in their marketing efforts—not less.

What will matter most, and be cost effective, is for businesses to innovate so as to keep their already valuable customers satisfied. Those that do it best will gain the most in the current uncertain economic climate. They will also be the ones who win in the long-term when the downturn eases. A strengthened customer base will provide the best platform to springboard into a commanding market lead.

Digital marketing allows businesses to develop far deeper levels of customer interaction while also providing accountable evidence of value.

Digital marketing provides one of the best ways of keeping the customer/business relationship alive. Marketers need to convince their chief financial officers (CFOs) of the ongoing need to engage their customers. This means being willing to do things differently. Hence, the winners will be those who are ready to talk to their customers in a new way. Customers will not be happy with being 'talked at' and so businesses that rely solely on one-way broadcast communication will lose out. Digital marketing allows businesses to develop far deeper levels of customer interaction while also providing accountable evidence of value.

Todays marketers recognise that consumers are savvy and have high expectations. With the proliferation of digital technologies, the roll-out of broadband and the growth of user-generated content (UGC), marketers have learnt that audiences are not just passive receptors but also active participants in marketing. As customers, we do not all react in the same way to broadcasted messages. For businesses, mass communication is no longer straightforward.

Communication channels—from cable television in the 1980s to the internet in the 1990s—have become more and more fragmented. As channels and choices multiply, so do differences in consumer behaviour. Marketers have had to adapt to this increasing fragmentation. Their methods can no longer simply be worked out and applied top-down. Going forward, marketers will need to embrace new channels and methods of communication that get closer to the customer through dialogue and engagement.

In this age of increased choice, customer expectations run high and businesses are damned if they fail to meet them. This is a lesson that marketers need to learn, especially during an economic downturn. As Nick Evans, a consultant with the digital marketing firm Jaywing, puts it: '[E]volved "dialogue" marketing needs to focus on making sure the customer can "pull" information and messages where they want, when they want, through the channels they want.'[2]

Marketers need a better understanding of consumer behaviour, something that can be worked out from consumers' history of choices and preferences. Here digital is vital: it

EXPERIENCE OF RECESSIONS

According to a recent PriceWaterhouseCoopers survey, CEOs' confidence about prospects for business have declined for the first time since 2003, alongside this, the fear of a global recession has emerged as the major threat to growth.[3]

CEOs have an average age of 50 in Europe[4] (52 in the top FTSE 100[5]), meaning that their earliest experience of working life (1980, if they started age 22) was dominated by recession, whereas their career development would have taken place in an era of boom, from age 34 to 50. In more dynamic sectors, like advertising, CEOs are commonly under 50 and the average age of a sales and marketing director is 39.[6] The managerial staff are aged around 40.[7] But in advertising, the average age of an account manager is just 26.[8]

Back in 2002, Hamish MacRae wrote: 'Most professional and managerial workers in the US aged under 40 have little practical experience of recession. Do the sums: someone born in 1961 and entering the workforce at the age of 22 would have started work in 1983. The only recession they will have known was the little one in 1990/1.'[9]

Today's, managers under 40 were born after 1968 and started work around 1990. Starting from a slough, their careers have been dominated by recovery and growth. In Britain, the economy grew solidly for 67 quarters since 1993. Moreover, many of those who lost out in the 1990 recession, retired and did not come back in the boom (see *One World Ready or Not*, by W. Greider, 2000).

So for most managers, the only experience of economic crash was the IT bubble of 2000—and that was restricted in its impact. No doubt many of those who lived through it would disagree, but that is because they have little to compare it with.

is the best tool for analysing and developing customer engagement. This is especially important as we can tailor messages and talk to customers in lots of different places, making every conversation more valuable. This dialogue can help businesses provide value 'that's totally relevant to [customers'] needs, and which acts to solidify their relationship with the brand'.[10]

Talking with customers is certainly the way to go, but it does mean more work. This doesn't mean that digital marketing is not cost effective—it is! But keeping the dialogue with the customer alive also means a lot more effort. And serving them with interactive content will raise their expectations.

In short, you have to be ready to support everything you promise. As Michael Nutley, editor-in-chief of *New Media Age*, has pointed out, 'once you've given people a service as part of your marketing effort, how do you move on and do something new?' If the commitment isn't maintained, 'you're left with the prospect of having to continue to support all these services or risk alienating your customers'.[11]

You have to be ready to support everything you promise.

Dove: Engaging real women

Unilever's Dove soap brand capitalised on making a deeper impact on women's lives than the soap alone could ever achieve. Dove was launched in 1992 and maintained a good sales level, but in 2004 it created a marketing sensation on a budget of £2.4 million.

Its central premise was a challenging take on preconceived ideas of 'beauty'. The above the line (ATL) activity featured ordinary women of all shapes and sizes, and asked customers to participate in a debate on the nature of beauty with the aim of improving female self-esteem. A new website, campaignforrealbeauty.co.uk, was created and has generated millions of visits to-date, with 50% of traffic coming from the UK.

Dove provided a platform for users to share experiences and to understand that the issues that contemporary women face are global.

This traffic was driven in part virally, but also as a result of a thoroughly integrated campaign incorporating ATL, on-pack promotion, sales promotion and strong PR pushes to women's magazines. The website itself has many levels of engagement—from activism to establishing authority. Visitor experience includes:

- Join the fund—make a donation to help charities improve women's self esteem.
- Engage with an interactive report—an online report reveals how women across the world perceive their own beauty. Participants are asked to double guess the answers.
- Nominate your own candidate who demonstrates real beauty.

Dove offers a truly interactive experience to challenge preconceptions about 'beauty'

A further part of the campaign featured a video hosted on YouTube showing the actual work that goes into creating a fashion photo shoot, including staggering levels of image manipulation. Even more impressive is the number of viewers—a cool 6 million. Endorsement of such an engagement strategy comes from the sheer number of people participating and the enthusiasm with which they do so. In this regard, the quotes from participants speak for themselves, like this one from Rita Barros: 'Beauty is an attitude that comes from within; from an optimism and belief in life.'

For Dove customers, there was a very genuine sense of added value through this campaign. Dove provided a platform for the users to share experiences and to understand that the issues that contemporary women face are global. The website gave women the space to have a voice and to gain support and inspiration. This approach will have brokered a deeper relationship between brand and consumer.

As a result of this combined activity, Dove became a national talking point. The effect on sales was phenomenal: a 700% increase in sales made it number three in the body lotions market in 2005, ahead of fierce competition from L'Oreal, Garnier and Olay. The campaign was re-invigorated at the end of 2007 and continues today. It is contributing to Dove's dominance in the marketplace, as well as having a resonance in the lives of many women.

www.campaignforrealbeauty.co.uk

CHAPTER 2
The changing face of the customer

The changing face of the customer

Consumers want to make their own choices and to establish their individuality through those choices. When it comes to what they buy, how they decorate their homes and what they drive, individuality matters. Therefore, it should also matter to those who want to sell to them.

Because individuals place so much importance on what they consume, they demand more from the process of consumption: from initial research, to transacting and after-sales care and support. Technology—in all its forms—has contributed to raising expectations of what is possible. And while customers are careful about what they want, they also want to know that they agree with the values of the companies with which they interact.

Customers want to know that they agree with the values of the companies with which they interact.

This is why today's consumers demand more; more interaction, more communication, more dialogue and more engagement with businesses. Brands that do not communicate their values openly won't survive when others embrace the new challenges of how to relate to their target audience.

The following trends indicate what we think are critical factors that digital has helped to develop, and will provide the means to resolve.

Trend one: Increased competition

One of the great benefits of digital media is that it has opened up global and local markets that were previously out of reach to many businesses. At the same time it has created markets that previously were either minute or non-existent. Chuck Rozanski of *Mile High Comics,* the largest comics retailer in the world, states that before the internet, the dwindling market in vintage comics led many to forecast the end of the industry. Today, *Mile High Comics* is a multi-million pound company and the demand for old comics has sky rocketed simply because of the visibility and availability that the web has offered through online stores like ebay.

But the opening up and creation of new markets has also increased competition. The barriers to entry into these old and new markets have crumbled. Today, a start-up with a new website and access to a supply and distribution chain can immediately make an impact where previously only a major sales force could have done so. Switching costs in almost all markets have dramatically lowered as more and more business is done online.

Every business and brand is now competing for the attention of our respective target audiences, and nowhere does this pose more difficult challenges than in digital media where the next interesting draw on a customer's attention is always just a click away. We live in the most attention demanding, fast-paced, information and product rich world that human beings have ever known.

The website Moneysupermarket.com coined the term WILFing (What was I Looking For?) to describe the effect that abundant choice online, and the accompanying distraction, has on consumers as they bounce around between websites, partially reading something before they move on to the next 'shiny trinket'.

In these circumstances, maintaining an active, engaged customer base that is not only loyal but might even become your advocate can prove invaluable.

BUSINESSES CUTTING BACK

'Marketing spend fell by more in the last quarter of 2007 than at any time in nearly two years', according to Bellwether.[12] As businesses draft their budgets for the coming year, caution about future sales prospects will tempt finance managers to hold down expenditure. That is a self-fulfilling prophecy. Market expectations pass from hunch to reality when budgets are set. Your customers are making decisions today about whether to go on buying your services or goods tomorrow.

When businesses spend money, they are, more often than not, buying from other businesses. Tight budgets will reduce overall spending. When businesses save money on the wage bill, they take more demand out of the system. The virtuous circle of growth gives way to a vicious circle of recession.

When business leaders like Michael Grade, Executive Chairman of ITV plc say that we are talking ourselves into a recession that is what they mean. It cannot be helped, though. Companies that fail to prepare for tighter markets will not survive on optimism.

Trend two: Media fragmentation

Once upon a time, 17 million people in the UK used to sit down in front of the television to watch *Coronation Street* at 7.30pm on a Wednesday evening. The ad-break at 7.45pm provided a unique opportunity for advertisers to reach a ready-made mass audience.

With the growth of the internet and new media, however, there has been an explosion of different channels, offering lots of opportunities to find, talk to, and engage, customers. The effect has been profound. People no longer rely just on television, radio and newspapers for news; or depend solely on the telephone to keep in touch with friends and families.

Tips

How to convince your CFO to fund the projects you want

1 **Don't just identify three killer reasons why you deserve funding.** You also need to build a wall of benefits. Try to think of 101 benefits your project could bring.

2 **Create case studies/stories of successes.** Success breeds success and quickly takes on mythic proportion within businesses. Use this to communicate the value of your activities.

3 **Select what you are prepared to cut and then propose your own cuts first.** As well as displaying prudence and acknowledging the need for a tightly run ship, it will help you identify which are the projects you should stand by and choose the battles to fight.

4 **Get the CFO to meet customers.** It is difficult to imagine what value the promised engagement offers and delivers unless you see it in the customers' eyes.

5 **Clearly display cause and effect:** If we invest X, we'll get Y results. However, if we invest X+A, we will get Y+B results.

6 **Know the CFO's pet hates.** They all have one – the website home page, a particular campaign, the intranet – and avoid discussions on this.

7 **Make the CFO your champion.** Make sure he/she can re-articulate the activities you're proposing and the benefits they will bring. A proud CFO who conveys his enthusiasm for your activities is worth all the effort.

8 **No big surprises.** Start talking to the CFO now. Make him/her your friend.

However, these changes are far from complete; the growth in new forms of communication has meant that many of us are only just beginning to find the best ways to stay in contact with each other—or even to find out what others whom we value are interested in and think. The choices seem infinite. The challenge for marketers is to be able to interact and engage through the right channels. Relying on customers to come to us is not enough. The challenge is knowing where they are, what they are doing and going out to engage them.

Trend three: Community and audience diversity

The internet has helped people explore and share more interests, hobbies and even purchasing choices than in any previous time. Without it a lot of niche interests, for instance, would remain undeveloped.

Online social networks have exploited and exploded what many have traditionally done privately or in exclusive settings: from book clubs to discussion groups, music sharing and local neighbourhood networks. Teenagers create their own domains and many learn computing long after retirement, proving that the appeal of digital disregards 'expected' ability.

Although much of the online activity on social networking sites like Facebook, MySpace and Bebo reflects real-world associations and networks, they do point to a greater breadth of diversity in activities, interests and associations. This is a huge opportunity for businesses to engage with customers with more meaningful content, products and services.

> How audiences understand themselves and their consuming preferences is a constantly evolving process.

PROVIDE DEEP LEVELS OF SERVICE

Providing customer self-service should be a cornerstone of continued and healthy business-customer relationships. First, it recognises the growing impatience of customers who will be more sensitive when things are not readily available. Ironing out the initial difficulties of setting up, installing and getting the most out of products and services can be time consuming and difficult, and can even cause customers to question the merits of their purchase.

Providing more stories, examples and commonly asked questions online means that, in most cases, customers can explore at their own leisure how to get the most out of their purchase. Well maintained, written and presented customer service areas will greatly endear customers to the brand, making them think 'they've thought of everything'. Conversely, there is nothing worse than having to figure out where to start or who to ask in order to get something working well.

Put simply: if businesses want to interact with customers using digital media, they will have to work out how to deal with an audience that is diverse, not uniform. A higher degree of sophistication is needed in order to create value and to attain enough credibility to be part of what interests today's target markets.

Trend four: Changing our consumption of information

Linear and print-based consumption of media is being challenged by the diversity of content online and digital interaction. It is questionable whether the humble book will ever be replaced, but one thing is certain: how we consume ideas has been revolutionised by digital communication.

Online publishers should not assume that readers are willing to follow a straight narrative from beginning to end, patiently waiting for a conclusion. Online browsers are not easy to control. Hypertext means we often skip to the end, while a culture of fast-forwarding means that, whether we are viewing video, listening to music or a Podcast, we tend to simply skip whatever does not immediately interest us.

Our expectations, demands and modes of interacting with content are no longer straight-forward and predictable. We can consume, interact and engage at our own convenience, that is to say, where and when we want. Higher expectations mean customers demand to have everything their way, on their own terms.

Trend five: Trusting authority and the opinion of others

When people refer to internet sources to help them make the right choices, they are deferring to others to make their choices for them. Often we call on the authority of those who we believe share our interests and values. But because of the infinite number of communication platforms online, working out which is useful can be hard work. The growing number of websites that provide user-generated content and recommendations, reviews and ratings have become important when making individual decisions as to what is valuable.

At the same time, expert opinion is also more sought after in the face of so much choice. As the *Guardian's* Jemima Kiss puts it, 'values of credibility and trust are more important than ever in the ocean of information we have to navigate every day. The technology is not enough on its own, and that should be a comfort to editors everywhere'.[13]

Trend six: Expect detail, not just brand

In some ways, the internet has prolonged our buying decisions. Intense market competition for our attention means that customers demand more—including options,

Monopoly: Advance to 'go'

Monopoly has distinct and warm associations for many British households. But it faced a challenge as it approached its seventieth anniversary with a sales plateau. Monopoly needed to reconnect with the British public and operate in a contemporary gaming environment.

The response to the challenge was to create an online experience that would bring the new updated version of Monopoly to life (including the addition of fresh London locations such as Soho). Research had demonstrated that families still loved Monopoly and were excited with the new choice of locations.

The game was replicated on the streets of London. On-line gamers were asked to choose a real life cabbie whose taxi was located via Global Positioning Satelight (GPS). Every time they went past their own property, the gamers got points, and they lost points if they went past a property owned by other players. Games took place over a 24-hour period and prizes were awarded every week.

The game is free to play after registration, and this became a great email list builder for Hasbro, Monopoly's manufacturer, to promote its product. Prominent 'invite a friend' options also bolstered the viral capacity of this game.

The approach made innovative use of media and communications and became a real online phenomenon generating a lot of 'buzz' around the activity.

During the launch period, the Monopoly website received 1 million visitors, with 190,000 playing the online game three times on average. What's more, 100,000 opted to receive future promotions. £2 million worth of PR activity was generated, and sales picked up significantly. They have subsequently risen by 30% year on year.

Hasbro provided a genuinely engaging online experience that relates to the real-life streets of London as well as re-invigorating interest in an established brand.

Monopoly combines online gaming with real-life taxi drivers to boost sales

www.www.monopolylive.com.co.uk

specifications, details and comparable offers. Customer support will be one important element for customers trying to decide whether the values of the brand fit with their outlook.

Businesses, then, need to be both more inventive and transparent in order to satisfy us. As one recent report on the experience of car manufacturer websites showed, it's not enough to talk brand and experience: we want the detail.

Global Reviews surveyed 1,000 UK consumers in November 2007 about their car buying. The outcome was clear. Car manufacturers have got it wrong online, misunderstanding how we use digital. Adam Goodvach, director of Global Reviews UK writing in *New Media Age*, put it simply: '[Car manufacturers] sought to transfer the brand and driving experience into an online format. This, however, goes against what customers are seeking from the websites. The importance of the brand is only fifth for new-car buyers and eighth for used-car buyers.'[14]

Today, with harsher competition for customers' cash, the devil is in the detail. Getting it right will influence buying decisions when brands understand what consumers want.

Moving towards an online customer engagement strategy

Creating an online customer engagement strategy can take time. Different types of organisations are more agile and flexible than others. The difficulty comes when confronted with a financial downturn. At that point, marketing and customer service departments tend to be given a contradictory message: make cuts and make the most of existing customers. In other words, you've got to do more but we're going to give you less money to do it.

As customer retention guru Jim Novo says: 'I know that when we get into a [...] recessionary market my phone rings more and I work a lot harder. The 'new client' customer retention business is counter-cyclical; people always wake up [...] and say "Hey, if we can't drive new customer volume, maybe we can sell more to existing customers!" You know, the CEO or somebody read that somewhere...

The problem with this kind of thinking is, in most cases, it's already too late to do anything about customer retention. That's not something people generally want to hear. I then say, "The economy is cyclical. Do you want to be prepared for the next downturn?"'[15]

Like all good things, customer retention, brand loyalty and customer evangelism have to be earned over time. But this doesn't mean that that there is nothing to gain from focusing on customer engagement now. Indeed, the virtue of adopting digital media as the interface for your customer interactions is that it can accelerate the building of deeper, more productive and more measurable customer relationships. During previous economic downturns we had none of this potential because digital media largely did not exist.

Winners and losers in past recessions

Below are the main causes and effects of the major recessions in the last 100 years. While many companies went to the wall, others flourished.

Year	1929	1973	1981	1991	2000
How bad, 1-10?	9	6	7	4	1.5
What happened?	After the US stock market crashed, the US economy slumped, factories closed and prices collapsed worldwide	After the US ended fixed exchange rates because it was reluctant to go on funding its European competitors, oil prices rose creating inflation and reducing output ('Stagflation')	US Federal Reserve chairman Paul Volker raised interest rates, signalling that America would no longer buy the world out of recession	Deutsche Bank put up interest rates to stop inflation after German reunification, exposing the credit-based boom, just as the Reagan recovery ran out of steam in the US	A credit-driven stock market climb overshot, investors having ignored shares' price/earnings ratios' until panic suddenly sorted the wheat from the chaff
Winners	Armaments, Chemicals (ICI), anc later Automobiles (Ford), Aerospace (Lockheed), America, the USSR	Saudis, nationalised industries (and 'national champions')—Rolls Royce, Chrysalis records, Robert Maxwell, trade union militants	Microsoft, Retail (the Body Shop, Sock Shop, Curries), Rupert Murdoch, Sky TV, Essex traders, McDonalds	IT, dotcoms, Yahoo, cable, the Creative Industries, Virgin, Manchester United	China, Apple, Gazprom, Green businesses (renewable energy, organic food) agri-business, biotech, the fine Art Market, home-owners, Google
Losers	Farmers, horsepower, minorities (Jews and black Americans), the City of London, the British Empire	Tyneside shipbuilders, UK textiles, Beckton Gasworks, family firms, the middle classes	IBM, Nationalised firms (British Steel, Leyland, NCB), trade unions, the City Gent, the North of England, the Third World, Clive Sinclair	The South of England, home-owners, the professional middle classes, Ratners, Robert Maxwell, the USSR	Boo.com. Go.com, Arthur Andersen, GEC, ICI, traditional advertising outlets (print and television), Enron, Marks and Spencer
How did it end?	Roosevelt's New Deal government purchases stabilised the American economy; world war and the Marshall Plan laid the basis of the recovery	The world market continued its roller coaster ride, with sudden slumps and booms right through to the 1980s	Financial deregulation helped stoke a boom and the retail sector grew as manufacturing contracted	Wage moderation, inward migration and the expansion of investment to the post-Communist world created extensive, job-rich growth	Central banks held down interest rates, and easy money migrated from stocks to houses and fine art

CHAPTER 3
Creating an online customer engagement strategy

Creating an online customer engagement strategy

Defining engagement

Our definition of customer engagement is: **Repeated interactions that strengthen the emotional, psychological and physical investment a customer has in a brand (product or company).**[16]

The two most important words here are 'repeated' and 'investment'. There is a widespread recognition of the importance of customer experience (often referred to as 'user experience' within digital media) for business and customer management.[17] A positive and satisfying customer experience is a prerequisite for engagement, but customer engagement can only take place after a number of satisfying experiences.

Those wishing to establish engaged relationships with customers and clients have to deliver positive and satisfying experiences more than once. For those who have traditionally been focused on brand awareness and customer acquisition, this is one of the hardest elements of engagement to come to terms with. Acquiring new prospects is hard enough but retaining them means even more work.

The investment a customer makes in a brand is also central to the concept of engagement. This investment can be on a highly emotional or psychological level where attachment to a brand can at times even seem almost irrational. Images broadcast of customers waiting in line for hours to be the first to collect a shiny new iPhone testify to the powerful emotional attachment many have for Apple products. The video sharing website YouTube has numerous videos of Apple customers just opening the product boxes to reveal their treasured new laptop.

But emotional attachments exist on many levels and can be equally powerful without being so high-profile. The negative reaction of some users of Flickr, the photo-sharing community website, to the news that Microsoft might acquire it is an excellent example of how an emotional and material (many people have thousands of their photos saved on the site) investment in a website demonstrates a high level of engagement with a brand.

It is important to recognise that customer engagement places conversions—the ultimate goal of marketing—into a longer term, more strategic context and is premised on the understanding that a simple focus on maximising conversions can, in some circumstances, decrease the likelihood of repeat conversions. The pushy sales person will gain a sale, but the store will lose a customer.

Understood in this way, it should be clear that the long-term goal of customer engagement is to encourage loyalty and even advocacy from the customer. As such, your level of customer engagement is the best indicator of how your business will fair in any economic downturn. Indeed, regardless of prevailing economic conditions, it is probably

Customer engagement places conversions into a longer term, more strategic context

fair to say that an engaged relationship is really your only cast iron guarantee of profitable future performance.

Who needs online customer engagement anyway?

Armed with our definition and understanding of what engagement is, it is now worth exploring for whom customer engagement is valid. Do we want to engage every customer? Can we engage every customer? The answer to both questions is 'no'.

So how do we decide who to focus on? The answer lies not in our businesses but with our customers. Try turning things around and look at engagement from your customer's point of view. The questions would then be: Why should I engage with your company? What's in it for me?

Below, we have outlined some reasons why your business might want to create an engaged customer base. We have explained some of the motivations for believing that engagement is something that your customers want.

The business imperative for online customer engagement

The cScape/E-consultancy second Annual Online Customer Engagement Survey, conducted in November 2007, showed that 77% of companies believed the importance of online customer engagement had increased over the previous 12 months. When asked what best described their organisation's interest in online customer engagement, 33% selected deepening and enriching their product or service offering, 32% chose reducing acquisition costs and increasing conversions, 21% said strengthening customers' emotional investment in a brand and 15% chose a need to adjust to the increased importance and power of the customer.

> An engaged relationship is really the best indicator a business has of future performance.

The survey illustrated how companies believe they have benefited from customer engagement initiatives over the past year:[18]

- Improved customer loyalty—43%
- Increased revenue—43%
- Enhanced their public standing—28%
- Reduced marketing costs—24%
- Gained bigger market share—16%
- Reduced customer service costs—16%
- Increased profits—14%
- Improved employee satisfaction—9%
- Improved business predictability—8%

What would your one practical tip be to a company/client on how to use digital to be a winner during a recession?

We know that marketing spend generally drops during a downturn. Companies cut back on marketing because they feel like they are 'pushing on a string'. Perhaps they cancel or stop buying advertising, or fire salespeople. But this is the wrong move. Actually, buying more marketing during a downturn to 'grab share' can have some positive effects.

But while companies should invest in more marketing, they shouldn't do so across the board. They should buy the right marketing, the marketing that generates the best quality customers.

They should reallocate marketing resources away from generating low value customers towards generating high value customers. If you know that trade shows generate leads which turn into high value customers, and that online ads generate leads that turn into low value customers, you should take the money you spend online and book more trade shows. You let go of salespeople that generate low value customers and use that salary to boost salespeople generating high value customers.

Of course, this analysis and planning is an exercise that should be done all the time, not just when entering a downturn. A business should always be trying to understand where customer value comes from and how it is created. But unfortunately, this issue most often comes up going into a downturn.

Jim Novo is the Co-Chair of the Web Analytics Association's Education Committee and is an interactive customer retention and loyalty expert. www.jimnovo.com

Monitor search volumes and pay per click (PPC) prices on a daily basis and reduce your bids as other advertisers fall by the way side. Otherwise you may find yourself paying over the odds as over inflated rates will drop with a fall in advertiser demand.

Leverage your content more. Media budgets will come and go, but content is king in Search. In a troubled economy, consumers may favour the natural results over the sponsored.

Consider more organic search marketing tactics to raise your content ranking in the search results. Equally, consumers will favour what they perceive as editorial vs advertorial as their propensity to purchase is reduced during tougher times. Focus less effort on the overt sell and more on offering advice, and your brand will be perceived more favourably.

Take advantage of the free technologies and applications that Google and the other search engines offer. These include free database uploads to Google's Local Business Center (for local or national retailers or services) and Google Analytics (website analytics software).

Trial the search engines' content networks as a more cost efficient way of running a broad reach advertising campaign. Google's AdSense network, for example, has an 80% reach of UK internet users, so in traditional media terms you can now target more pairs of eyes through these networks than you can through terrestrial TV or national press. Ads are contextually relevant so wastage is minimal, and you control the rate you pay on a keyword/theme level.

Amanda Davie is Head of Search at i-level. www.i-level.com

With so many benefits to customer engagement being identified and experienced at the moment, it is hard to ignore the role it can play for businesses. An engaged relationship is really the only indicator a business has of future performance. Digital media allow for customer experiences to be truly engaging, interactive, memorable and highly measurable, something that has always proved difficult in the more traditional media.

As indicated in this year's Online Customer Engagement Survey, the potential to reduce a reliance on costly customer acquisition can be a key benefit of engagement. In a contracting market, competition for a constant supply of new customers can be incredibly costly and resource intensive. An engaged customer is both less likely to defect and to be less price conscious, because he or she values the emotional connection with that particular brand over all others.

Realising practical and emotional needs

While specific customer requirements are wide and varied, the general requirements of all customers are not that difficult to identify. These fall into two broad categories—practical needs and emotional needs. Practical needs might include simplicity, ease of use, availability of customer support, a cheap price and that the product or service is fit for purpose. Emotional needs are how the customer feels about the way the practical needs are realised. In addition, customers bring many other emotional needs to the customer/brand relationship.

Every time a customer interacts with a business there is some level of emotional need present. More often than not, this need is either marginalised or unrecognised and is then left undeveloped in favour of concentrating on servicing the practical needs. These dual needs interact and mutually reinforce each other. For example, the desire not to feel that you have been taken advantage of, or ripped off, if you like, is an emotional need based squarely on factors like practical utility and comparison with other products and services.

Satisfaction is no indicator of future performance

Customer satisfaction should not be confused with engagement. Satisfying experiences are essential to building engagement but satisfaction is merely an indicator of your past performance. Without engagement, the value of satisfaction to a company can be low to non-existent. For example, satisfaction scores in the US motor industry are incredibly high with 90% of customers reporting that they are satisfied or very satisfied. However, repurchase rates are only around 40-50%.[19]

During an economic downturn an emphasis on satisfaction can actually be quite damaging to a company as it can distract attention from the more valuable process of developing forms of customer engagement replete in emotional attachments.

Greenpeace: Green to the core

Greenpeace galvanised support through complex tagging and blogging techniques.

Greenpeace, the campaigning environmental charity used the very latest in social networking channels to pressure the global computer giant Apple.

The web, due to the speed with which it disseminates information, plus its cost effectiveness and limited carbon footprint is the perfect springboard for guerrilla campaigning. In 2007, Greenpeace launched an intelligent pressure campaign against Apple. Instead of setting polarised debates, depicting Apple as the villain, it acknowledged Apple's popularity but pointed out its current environmental deficiencies. This was encapsulated in their strapline: 'If you love Apple like we do, don't you wish it would go green?'

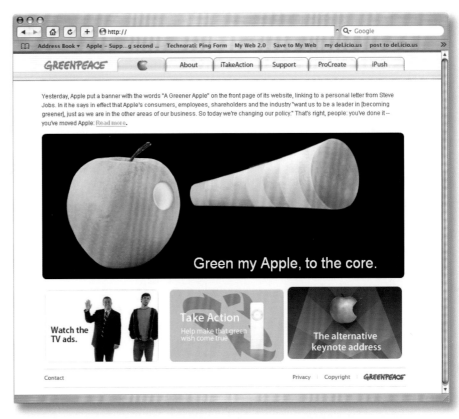

Greenpeace spoofs Apple's image to broker powerful online campaigning

www.greenmyapple.com

Greenpeace was using 'Apple-like' language to show empathy rather than confrontation in order to encourage a review on policies and attitudes.

Behind this challenge was a well-researched study, with Greenpeace scoring companies from one to 10 in terms of their environmental efficiency. Of the featured companies, Apple scored a feeble 2.5.

The call to action was classic Greenpeace—humour and immediacy: 'Tell Steve Jobs to go green to the core.'

Thousands responded and Greenpeace made the campaign enjoyable and easy to join, with a pre-populated message that would be submitted once respondents' details were completed.

As the campaign built momentum, former US vice president Al Gore got involved and a new website, GreenMyApple.org, was set up. It was playfully designed spoofing Apple's own image.

Greenpeace provided a set of tools including buttons and banners so supporters could personalise content on their own social networking and blogging websites. Campaigning was made easier and looked cohesive, encouraging links to go back to the main website, boosting search engine rankings and gave the campaign real momentum.

Mac users were encouraged to hug their macs and paste the images on Flickr. Tapping into the creative interests of apple users, Greenpeace also suggested they make their own t-shirts and videos, and publish the results online.

The combined efforts proved a potent mix. Apple has vowed to become greener, and Greenpeace will no doubt keep the pressure on.

The call to action was classic Greenpeace —humour and immediacy.

CHAPTER 4
How to create your own online customer engagement successes

How to create your own online customer engagement successes

If having a customer engagement strategy makes good business sense during a boom period, then it is even more important during a period of economic turbulence. As the economy slows, perhaps starts contracting even, customers become more selective regarding whom they do business with and how they make their buying decisions. Add to this both the fact that your competitors are vying for your customers' attention and your own need to streamline operations, and you have a heady cocktail that can lead businesses to lose sight of some of the key elements of their engagement strategy.

Below we have highlighted what we believe are the three most important considerations that need to be embedded in your customer engagement strategy and planning. Neglect any of these as a result of an economic slow-down and it's more than likely that your business will also be neglected by consumers.

One: Multi-channel right-touching

Concentrating on your most productive channels and cutting back resources where they appear to be least productive—e.g. emphasising your printed catalogue over your email newsletters, or your search marketing over your social media presence—might well be many businesses' first choice of cut-backs in an economic downturn. But there are two important reasons why businesses should question this approach.

Firstly, there is always something to be said for a contrary strategy. Many of your competitors are likely to adopt a similar approach, that is, rationalising their resources and focusing on just a few media channels. This can mean that there are greater dividends to be won from doing the opposite.

Secondly, our customers live in a multi-channel world, and so should we. While a customer might buy through a catalogue or a website, it is highly likely that other channels contribute significantly to both their product awareness and purchasing decision. While the practice of defining customer journeys is popular in the user experience industry, we prefer the concept of the Customer Odyssey.[20] This phrase captures the often quite complicated way that customers first discover, then learn about and purchase any product or service over an extended period of time, through multiple channels and encounters.

When it comes to customer retention and engagement, a multi-channel approach can be even more essential. Email, phone, website, blog, social media, high street presence etc are all valuable channels that your customer might choose—and expect—to access in order to interact with a brand and other customers. By excluding or limiting your presence in any channel you are reducing your ability to engage with the single 'scarce productive resource' that can deliver business growth.

There is always something to be said for a contrary strategy.

When it comes to customer engagement, a multi-channel approach is essential.

THE FUTURE OF ADVERTISING

Advertising will probably remain a healthy business in 2008—even if the economic trends say otherwise. As Sir Martin Sorrell, CEO of WPP points out, the combined effects of the Beijing Olympics, the European Football championship and the US elections will make 2008 profitable and 'could add as much as 1% of additional growth to advertising expenditure.'[21] But the following year will be tougher with no major events to rely upon. Still, across the board, on both sides of the Atlantic, advertising will prove more resilient than many think, bolstered in the main by the impact of the internet. As the Economist put it: '[The] internet has brought greater accountability to advertising. Marketing chiefs can now prove that a click on an online ad produces a sale.'[22]

Traditional print and television advertising struggle to justify exact returns and value. But while internet advertising proves more accountable, it is still expensive. Social media applications like Facebook, MySpace and Bebo that have attracted millions of prime audiences look like a good place to work.

As Josh Bernoff of Forrester Research put it: '[S]ignificant ad campaigns cost millions whereas social applications range from $10K to $200K depending on complexity… [S]ocial applications will be one of the primary advertisement channels of choice during a downturn.'[23]

Hence, as the Economist outlines, 'The internet's interactivity and wealth of product information make it the best means of generating short-term sales—whereas television is best for long-term brand-building.' This implies a split: digital is best suited to ride out a downturn, especially because of its measurable return, whereas offline advertising requires more investment and so is more likely to be used by those with bigger budgets. Smaller businesses can remain online, not least because measurability means it's easier to justify to shareholders.[24]

Once you have decided upon a multi-channel approach, how you use those channels becomes paramount. This is where the concept of 'right-touching' can help.

> As Dave Chaffey puts it, 'Right-touching is a multi-channel communications strategy customised for individual prospects and customers across a defined customer lifecycle. It delivers the right value proposition accompanied by the right message with the right tone at the right time with the right frequency and interval, using the right media/communications channels to achieve the right balance of value between both parties.'[25]

In other words, it is essential to find the most appropriate way to engage your customer. A key element of right-touching can be described as sense or respond. This means that you should look at every customer interaction or response to a communication and use that information to deliver relevant communications through the right combination of channels. In part, this process can be achieved through automation. If you notice a customer's email open rates are dropping, then cut back on emails and adapt the content to entice the recipient. If a customer accesses your website via a search engine, then personalise the landing page with links to content relating directly to the search term. Businesses that incorporate the concept of right-touching into their multi-channel engagement strategies will stand out from the crowd of businesses retreating in the face of economic pressure.

Two: Segmentation

Don't use segmentation to pigeonhole customers: use it to delight and surprise them.

In many ways segmentation needs to be understood as a necessary evil. Ideally we would want to talk to each customer individually in the appropriate language. Online, we are often once removed from direct contact with our customers. Even if we could talk to them individually, the resources and management required to do so would make it untenable. Segmentation allows us to group our customers into manageable chunks. The trick is to know how best to create these segments.

All too often businesses create their segments based on relatively fixed customer demographics; male, female, young, old, rich, poor. In almost all situations online this type of rigid segmentation is counterproductive leading to generalisations which fail to connect with customer interests. Customer engagement requires greater flexibility and responsiveness.

We are all complex, multifaceted individuals. What can be right for us one minute can seem wrong the next. Don't use segmentation to pigeonhole customers, use it to delight and surprise them. Base your segmentation around customer behaviour first. Treat the more engaged differently to the less engaged. Offer those who only infrequently visit your website a monthly email newsletter full of highlights. For regular visitors, provide weekly newsletters or regular alerts. Developing offerings for these behavioural segments ensures the availability of choice for all and allows customers to change their preferences according to their changing habits and interests.

Three: From monologue to dialogue

As the groundbreaking *The Cluetrain Manifesto*[26] stated, 'markets are conversations'. The language of business, like mission statements and brand superlatives, doesn't translate well to digital media where there is an assumption that everyone can have their say and that every opinion deserves space.

In order to have a human conversation, customers and businesses need both to listen and to talk. The development of any strategy focusing on customer engagement will need to find a place for customers to have their voice heard.

What would your one practical tip be to a company/client on how to use digital to be a winner during a recession?

As an ebusiness strategist and web analytics consultant, a couple of people asked me if I was worried about the impending economic turbulence. After thinking about it for five seconds, my answer was a loud no! In difficult times companies have no excuses for doing 'stuff' without measuring the outcomes. Moreover, they don't have excuses to do anything without first planning and setting realistic goals. If you are to spend $1,000 or $1Million on something you absolutely want to realise, leave emotions aside, forget about big technological and design overhaul and enter into a continuous improvement process with simple, measurable, achievable, realistic and short term objectives (yes, the good old SMART objective). In *Competing on Analytics*, Thomas H. Davenport identified a few steps toward an analytical culture: 1) find an executive partner 2) begin to build analytical skills 3) implement analytical technology 4) get your data in shape 5) examine your business strategy. If you haven't done this already, now is the time. In my opinion, smart objectives, continuous improvement, and an analytical culture are key elements not only to survive, but to be winners in a troubled economy.

Stéphane Hamel is an eBusiness Strategist and Web Analytics Consultant at Immeria. He is also an online instructor at The University of British Columbia.

blog.immeria.net

My one top tip to be a winner during an economic downturn is to focus on the processes by which you leverage web analytics. Instead of making you work for the data, make the data work for you. There is a well defined process that describes how you can translate data into information, information into insights, and insights into action. Implementing this process is the difference between measurement being an ongoing cost and being a source of profit.

Ask yourself these questions:

How much do high bounce rates affect your Return on Advertising Spend (ROAS) and what are you doing about it?

How engaged are your visitors and what value do highly engaged visitors bring to your business?

How satisfied are your customers and what is the net negative impact of poorly or unsatisfied visitors to your site?

Companies that 'get' web analytics and have invested in the process are far more likely to know the answers to these questions. Consequently, they will be confident in their ability to spend money wisely in the digital realm.

Eric Peterson is CEO of Web Analytics Demystified and author of *Web Analytics Demystified* and *Website Measurement Hacks*.

blog.webanalyticsdemystified.com/weblog

RSPB utilises dynamic survey techniques to reward and engage participants

www.rspb.org.uk/birdwatch

Royal Society for the Protection of Birds

The Royal Society for the Protection of Birds (RSPB) is the leading charity campaigning for and improving the environment of the UK's bird population. It has developed a clear, navigable website that combines information with activism.

As part of its campaigning and customer engagement approach, RSPB's website visitors are asked to take part in an annual online survey which asks participants to specify the types of birds that they see in their gardens.

This survey takes place annually and has proved popular as well as scientifically useful. In 2007, over 400,000 people took part, counting the birds in their garden for an hour. Together they spotted six million birds across 236,000 gardens, helping to reveal which species are thriving and which are declining in the UK.

For the RSPB, this has provided invaluable information to support its campaigning work and it has become a national event. Additionally, the RSPB has boosted its potential pool of supporters, donors and members. By using online survey techniques, the organisation has made good use of existing media and devices, such as dynamically illustrating the number involved in the survey to add to the customer engagement. And by collaborating online with likeminded peers, customers involved in the survey have found an outlet for their passion.

CHAPTER 5
The tactics for creating a customer engagement strategy

The tactics for creating a customer engagement strategy

Planning customer engagement methods might seem like a logical first step for a strategy but in reality we know that how our strategy is executed usually has a significant impact on reshaping our plans. One of the major challenges for all businesses, and for marketers in particular, has been the rapid development of technology, especially the pace of change in digital media.

As Matt Shobe, co-founder and chief design officer of Feedburner put it: 'The web keeps changing! The damn thing won't sit still for five minutes.'[27]

> The more relevant and satisfying the experiences we provide for our customers, the more likely they are to desire engagement with us.

Facebook, RIA, APIs, widgets, podcasting, MySpace, eCRM, Twitter, wikis, video, Ajax, Second Life, Silverlight, gadgets, RSS, blogs… It is easy to get swamped with the endless possibilities opening up before us, leading us to chase one dazzling jewel after another. The pressure to embrace the next opportunity can be immense, not least because each new development and digital offering really can present big benefits for those wishing to develop customer engagement.

Each business and marketer will assess their tactics and decide where to invest their resources best. Below, we have identified what we believe are the four most important considerations when planning your customer engagement tactics.

One: Personalisation and the rich experience

The more relevant and satisfying the experiences we provide for our customers the more likely they are to desire engagement with us.

Getting personal

An important element in any engaged relationship is recognition that your needs are catered for and well met. We all like to be listened to and responded to appropriately. More than any media before it, digital, and in particular the internet, has opened up the potential for niche marketing. Personalisation provides the opportunity for the ultimate in niche marketing: the ability to talk to each individual according to their needs, interests and contexts.

Any salesman worth his salt knows that the first step to selling anything is knowing something about your customer. The more you know about your customer and the better you can tailor your description of the benefits of the product or service you provide, the more compelling you brand will be. Digital media place the potential of personalisation firmly into the hands of every business.

Many are familiar with the Amazon personalisation process. If you have bought a book on a particular subject on Amazon, the site recommends something else that you might

EMOTIONAL ATTACHMENTS

The US based consulting firm Gallup has done extensive research into the emotional side of engagement and has identified four related perceptual components that build an overall emotional link, tying customers to a brand. These four perceptual components—confidence, integrity, pride and passion—are forged and shaped by a customer's experiences of a brand, product or service.[28]

Gallup's Brand Attachment relationship hierarchy.

Brand attachement: the foundation

Source: *Married to the Brand: Why Consumers Bond with some Brands for Life* by William McEwen.

The first two levels of brand attachment—confidence and integrity—are the basic emotional requirements for customer engagement, in other words, being able to meet a customer's expectations by delivering what has been promised and doing so consistently. Research published in January 2008 into reasons for customer churn rates identified 'not being recognised as a valuable customer' as the top reason for changing suppliers. The concept of being fairly treated (not to be confused with special treatment) goes straight to the heart of the integrity required for establishing the emotional requirements for engagement.

The upper two levels of Gallup's brand attachment hierarchy—pride and passion—refer to how the customer is made to feel about the relationship. Feeling valued, appreciated and personally respected are all critical elements of pride and can be felt by both customers and the brand. Also, it is important to understand that passion is not just something for a premium brand. In fact, the feeling of being unable to do without something can often be felt most intensely at the bottom end of the market.

Top tips for online marketing in a troubled economy

1   **Focus on current customers.** Kill two birds with one stone by concentrating on acquisition by referral. Build in viral advocacy to everything you do online.

2   **Reward loyalty.** Acknowledge that times might be tough for everyone and that you value the relationship you have. Pleasing customers doesn't have to be expensive, just surprising.

3   **Practice contrarian strategies.** Your competitors will be focusing on the basics and pulling back from lower ROI activities—you'll never have a better opportunity to get ahead of them.

4   **Think and act joined-up.** How about integrating your separate activities? Use your Pay Per Click (PPC) budgets to drive email newsletter sign-ups, for instance.

5   **Get faster.** Costs rise as projects and campaigns get bogged down in details. Reject perfection for fit-for-purpose and trial ideas using digital media first.

6   **Test, listen and measure.** Create opportunities to learn. Ask your customers, watch what they do and compare. Whether it's A/B testing or rapid prototyping, take advantage of digital's ability to make you smarter quickly and let your competitors retrench and get dumber.

7   **Don't reinvent the wheel.** The past few years have seen a plethora of new digital offerings that can offer what you need at a fraction of the cost. Why build your own video player when you can use YouTube? How about using free blogging software for your microsite?

8   **Don't assume too much.** Responses to economic problems are not pre-determined. Price isn't always a customer's main concern. Indeed, in some situations, extravagance can be a virtue. The entertainment industry - films, theme parks etc - normally do very well in troubled economies, so tap into a sense of fun and don't be too doom-laden.

be interested in either via email or the on the website next time you visit it. Being able to capture, retain and act upon the knowledge your organisation has of customers sounds simple, but in many cases the ability to connect backend computer systems containing purchase records and other useful and insightful details can be much harder than expected. Despite the fact that Amazon has had this type of personalisation in place for over a decade it is still relatively rare to see it practiced by other companies.

For many organisations the cost involved in planning and executing the sort of back end Customer Relationship Management (CRM) work that is required for extensive personalisation is a challenge at the best of times. In an economic downturn it becomes even more trying. However, this doesn't mean that personalisation should in anyway be rejected out of hand.

If anything, the importance of personalisation grows when the market is tougher. When customers are scarce, the importance of maintaining customer relationships becomes greater. At this point, then, personalisation can play a vital role in differentiating you from your competitors and building customer engagement.

> The importance of personalisation grows when the market is tougher.

If a fully integrated eCRM system is an unobtainable for you, then don't worry—there are many levels of personalisation that can deliver substantial results without the ultimate sacrifice of resources. Simply modelling you customers' behaviour can enable you to personalise effectively.

For example, one of the most productive models looks at your customers' life-stage and changes your content to fit with their appropriate position. So, for first time visitors, show them content different to that shown to those who've visited your website before. If it's the first time they've visited tell them properly who you are, explain what they can get from you that they can't get elsewhere, and do this on more than just your home page—many people will be visiting pages deep in your site straight from search engines.

Tell those who have previously visited your website what's new. If they're returning within a set time period, say a week, show them something related to what they looked at last time. This works on the assumption that they must have seen something vaguely interesting or they wouldn't have returned. Other models can be based upon which website sections your customers might have previously visited or where your visitors have come from. Personalising small areas of landing pages based on the key words that visitors search on can dramatically improve both one-off conversions and long-term engagement.

Getting interactive

One of the great defining features of digital media is the ability to provide interactive experiences for customers. While many have moved on from flat marketing content online (like brochure ware), there is still some way to go before most companies are creating the sort of engaging experiences that are likely to drive customers to return or to tell their colleagues and friends about it. In the past few years, there has been a dramatic increase in

What would your one practical tip be to a company/client on how to use digital to be a winner during a recession?

Set good business objectives, get the best web analytics system you can afford and measure the impact of your various marketing activities on those business objectives. If you're in retail and your objective is to increase sales, you need to be able to answer questions like: Which source of traffic generates the most sales? How does my shopping cart perform? How many people know about my products? What is my conversion rate?

If you're in business to business operations and your objective is to acquire more leads you need to be able to find answers to questions like: Which source of traffic generates the most leads? Which content is most useful to my prospects? How many people fill in our online forms? Do the incentives I give my visitors to become a lead for my business work? What is my conversion rate?

All of these questions, and a lot more, can be answered by web analytics tools. Of course you can get much more sophisticated than that by determining who your best chance of business is based on; loyal visitors or repeating visitors. Or you can cater more specifically for different target groups. The analytics tools available can greatly help you determine the answers to a lot of questions you may have and without them digital marketing is much less effective as you have to resort to guessing the answers.

Steve Jackson is working for Satama and serves as the International co-chair for the Web Analytics Association[39]

blackbeak.conversionchronicles.com

Sharpen your niche and build a digital community for it.

Ben McConnell is the co-author books *Citizen Marketers* and *Creating Customer Evangelists* and of the blog Church of the Customer

customerevangelists.typepad.com

At the onset of a recession, it is worth applying extra vigilance to your current segmentation models – they may need refining or the rules may need to change altogether.

The clues to segmentation change may be informed by observing customers, online behaviour. Set criteria such as monitoring email changes like open and click through rates, tracking which products and offers customers click through on, and what areas of the website are being visited.

Once refined, it is worth investing in the key customers, enticing the more price sensitive with special offers and providing added value and assurance of quality to the more affluent customers.

Companies do need to compromise and negotiate with their customer more when times are hard, but adapting approaches to the clues customers are giving you can broker good customer loyalty and maximise profitability.

Lucy Conlan, e-marketing consultant, cScape Customer Engagement Unit

www.cscape.com

Eliminate bullshit! People crave proper information about the products and services your business offers yet the vast majority of sites fail to deliver this basic level of support to their potential customers. Words are the most powerful weapon any organisation has, and online they count more than anywhere.

So why fill pages with marketing hyperbole that means nothing? Why are promotions forced onto consumers who have no known interest? Why are most descriptions of products totally rubbish? Product descriptions are either over the top, or totally devoid of useful information.

This is a description from a major UK mail order catalogue:

"Green And Gold Reactive Vase £35 Ceramic. H57cm. 361-462-X41"

Are you sold? Will you part with £35 based upon this rather sparse description and the accompanying basic image?

But shoving in lots of adjectives won't help either. Take, for example, a description of a hotel from a leading travel agent: "Set amongst beautiful landscaped gardens and with stunning views out to the crystal blue sea, the Sol Cayo Santa Maria enjoys an idyllic position directly on the white sand beach…"

Within the same section of the site, the word 'stunning' is used 107 times, 'beautiful' 170 times, 'crystal' 74 times and 'idyllic' 22 times! When all the descriptions contain the same adjectives the result is just noise, and it certainly doesn't help the consumer. The questions you have to ask are; who writes the copy on your website? Do they understand your customers or prospects? Are they writing to help people do research or simply to hype things up?

Start treating your customers like real people, not like abstract target audiences. Use the language they would use and work harder at being authentic.

Matthew Tod is founder and CEO of Logan Tod & Co.

www.logantod.com

Marketers spend 22% of their advertising dollars on TV and only 6% online. But while there's definitely an opportunity, don't think that just doing digital is the answer. You still need to be creative to stand out from the crowd. The technology can help with that through viral media but something becomes viral only because the content is good.

Steve Clayton is Chief Technology Officer of the UK Microsoft Partner Group and author of the blog A Geek in Disguise

blogs.msdn.com/steveclao1

Xovent Lisa? 15? the implementation of Rich Internet Applications (RIA) and the use of technologies and development languages like Ajax, Flash, Flex, AIR and Silverlight to deliver the features and functionality of more traditional desktop based applications through the web or on mobile devices.

This sort of interactivity really comes into its own when used for:

- Visualising and manipulating data e.g. maps and predictive calculators
- Showcasing important product features e.g. zooming photos and rotating products
- Enabling customers to configure products or services e.g. feature rich social networking sites like Facebook
- Streamlining multi-step processes e.g. simplifying forms and shopping baskets

Recent research from Forrester indicated that 52% of online consumers had used highly interactive applications like Google Maps. Even more will have encountered richer experiences, created with Ajax on sites like Facebook and the BBC. As our customers encounter these improved experiences on a more regular basis their expectations of what we should provide will rise. Our audience will migrate to whatever provides them with the opportunity to engage best through simple and rewarding experiences.

But will the business feel the value of the extra effort required to create these richer experiences? According the Forrester research, the answer is yes. Of the companies using RIA, 69%

RE-WRITE THE STORY TO RAISE EXPECTATIONS

What usually happens when customers have made a purchase is that after a while, they no longer remember or value the initial excitement or value that drove them to make the original purchase. Instead, their continued experience of using the product or service is overtaken by utility: does it keep performing its function well? While this is certainly no bad thing, awareness of the brand lessens.

But there is an opportunity to restate both those initial elements that drove the customer to make their choice and to show how the product (and its brand) have continually adapted to an ever-changing environment.

This aspect of developing a continual communications strategy is especially important for those products and services that provide information, knowledge and ideas. Without constant nurture, customers may develop misconceptions of continued value. In fact, with 'nearby' competitors trying to steal the limelight, the brand will need to restate itself more times than they realise.

said that the results were either equal to or exceeded their expected business impact. 10% expressed disappointment, while 21% hadn't measured the business impact.

At the core of developing customer engagement is the ability to deliver value through digital media in an anticipated, relevant and personal way. The use of personalised and richer experiences is important for achieving these goals.

FACEBOOK AND EMOTIONALISM

Why have so many people taken up social networking tools? It is easy to recognise a practical need to stay in touch with colleagues and friends. The ease of use of Facebook is undoubtedly one of the main reasons its use has sky rocketed in such a short time. But can practical aspects fully explain its popularity? Probably not. The popularity of Facebook can only be understood by recognising the emotional role it plays for its audience.

Dr BJ Fogg, of the Stanford University Persuasive Technology Lab, has commented on the emotional and psychological role that joining Facebook groups plays for people. Despite first appearances, these groups are rarely places for interaction.

Purpose #1: We express identity

Most people join Facebook groups to express who they are, where they are from, or what they like. By joining a group we get a label for our profile page; a group membership identifies a part of us; the list of groups shows our many facets.

Purpose #2: We show solidarity

Many people join a Facebook group to show support for a cause (or sometimes a person). In our groups we don't discuss the cause. That's not how things work here on Facebook. We just join the group and are happy to see the numbers increase.

Purpose #3: We make fun of ourselves

A significant number of groups seemed designed to make fun of themselves. They often have crazy titles, and by joining them we amuse our friends. Joining a group is like sharing a joke.

Two: Persuasion and the role of psychology

No business or customer has existed in such a demanding, fast-paced, information saturated and potentially confusing historical moment as we do today. Even when faced with the pressures and tough decisions necessitated by an economic slowdown, few of us are prepared to collect all the available data to sit down and make a totally rational decision. Instead, much of the decision making process is based on cues—the signs and impressions we gain from context and presentation. We use these cues, known as 'decisional heuristics', to take shortcuts in the decision making process.[29]

It is only in this context that we can understand the importance of persuasion. Persuasion is about creating and shaping these cues. By providing helpful short cuts we can aid our customers' understanding of the value and credibility of our offering and ultimately encourage them to take the actions we desire them to take. Online, these actions might include: completing a form, clicking a button and buying a product, returning to visit us or promoting us to friends and colleagues.

Credibility

Without credibility there is no customer engagement. Perceptions of credibility can result from firsthand experiences over time (earned), through third party endorsements, reports or referrals (reputed), through simple first impressions (surface), and via pre-existing impressions in the mind of the perceiver (presumed).[30] Many businesses believe that earned credibility is the most powerful, but each of the above can be telling. In fact, earned credibility can be the easiest to lose just through a single negative experience.

One inappropriate email from a company can considerably undermine a brands credibility despite previous useful and relevant communications.

An experiment conducted by the online journal *Marketing Experiments* in February 2007 increased conversion rates by over 12% simply by incorporating two of the credibility types above in a look and feel redesign.[31] The starting role for persuasion in online customer engagement is to increase credibility in the mind of our customers.

Influence

There are around 60 different persuasive techniques but in the mid-1980s, professor Robert Cialdini distilled them down to six weapons of influence:[32]

- Reciprocity

- Commitment & consistency

- Social proof

- Liking

- Authority

- Scarcity

While all of the above can be used to persuade and improve conversions, reciprocity, commitment together with consistency and liking can be immensely powerful tactics within a customer engagement strategy. When used well, each can deepen the customer relationship and encourage sustained interactions.

For example, a strategy integrating testimonials and UGC can lead to public demonstrations of commitment from customers, making it infinitely more likely that they will interact with you in the future.

Persuasion Windows

A key aspect of customer engagement is timing. Mistime a communication and your customers are more likely to think less of you, and then they will possibly even start to disengage. Conversely, get the timing right and make the content relevant, and engagement is far more likely to follow.

There are key moments within our interactions on- and offline when customers are more susceptible to persuasion and are more open to undertaking an action, making a connection or changing an opinion. These are our persuasion windows. If we don't interact and entice while the window is open it is likely to be harder to gain engagement later.

It is certainly possible to identify and wait for a persuasion window within the normal customer relationship. However, the real art is to encourage their opening. There are six recognised scenarios that can lead to the opening of a persuasion window:[33]

- when you are in a good mood
- when your worldview no longer makes sense
- when you can take action immediately
- when you feel indebted because of a favour
- immediately after you have made a mistake
- immediately after you have denied a request

The point of refusal—usually thought of as the ultimate in disengagement—does in fact momentarily open a window through which we can connect by offering alternatives and clarifying our online value proposition. Many of the most successful subscription-based websites understand the power of refusal and cultivate the opening of persuasion windows by explicitly denying access. Subscription only access is a good example of this, because it both incentivises non-subscribers to engage while reaffirming subscriber benefits.

Persuasion as a dialogue

The essence of digital is interaction. As the medium continues to develop, so we need to recognise that persuasion is a two-way process, a dialogue we should embrace within our customer engagement strategies. True customer centricity can only come when we facilitate and embrace the changes that our customers want to make both to our products and to us.

Probably the best understood example of the dialectics of persuasion is the Amazon system for adapting recommendations. By voting on the recommendations that Amazon's website makes to us, we can help improve those recommendations, improve Amazon's sales and improve our overall experiences.

Therein lays the value of persuasion. As the world increases in complexity and our ability to navigate it becomes more fraught, especially during an economic slowdown, the use of persuasion helps both businesses and customers. In this sense, mutual benefit is the foundation of customer engagement.

Three: Atomisation and the distributed experience

One of the major concepts of our Web 2.0 world that has been slightly hidden beneath the hype is that of content 'atomisation' and the accompanying concept of a distributed user experience (DUX).

'Atomisation', as it is used here, refers to a diaspora of content and functionality; the breaking down of your offering into bite sized portions that can be spread across multiple locations, even multiple channels. Gone are the days when every marketing activity you undertake should be designed to drive as much traffic as possible back to your own website. Instead of trying to control and corral our customers we should reach out and service them where they are:

> As Ashley Friedlein, CEO of E-consultancy puts it: 'If your customers spend 99% of their online time on sites other than your own perhaps you should focus on trying to be present where they are rather than paying a fortune to drag them to your site?'[34]

'Atomisation' refers to the breaking down of your offering into bite sized portions that can be spread across multiple locations.

This might mean providing some of your site's functionality free as a widget to a Facebook group or providing a feed that other companies can use on their website or intranet. While content syndication is far from a new idea, the traditional motivation was primarily to generate money. Today, however, content atomisation needs to be understood through the prism of engagement with your brand. It is worth spelling out the benefits that embracing an atomised approach to your content can provide.

- You can deliver value directly to your customer. In many cases you might even benefit from being situated in a more familiar and timely context, e.g. a customer's iGoogle home page.
- By having a presence for your content and brand on other websites you can reach an audience that might otherwise have never encountered you.
- You can build up content exchange relationships with other businesses and websites, enriching both your own website and delivering greater value to your website visitors.

• Links back to your site created through the atomisation of your content can deliver new customers to your site and improve your organic search engine optimisation.

Finally, it is worth mentioning that one of the biggest barriers to embracing the concept of atomisation is the fear of loss of control. It is true that once you allow others to use your functionality and content, you cannot be totally in control. But it is equally important to understand that we can never 'own' a customer, and in many cases don't even 'own' our own brand. Customers will discuss us and shape opinions about our products and services as they see fit. The question we need to answer is: Do we wish to join these discussions and help shape them by providing value to our customers, or would we rather stay at home guarding our brand?

Four: Social tools and the conversation

The Cluetrain Manifesto[35] asserted that unlike ordinary media, digital media enable people to have 'human-to-human' conversations, which can radically transform traditional business practices.

> 'A powerful global conversation has begun. Through the internet, people are discovering and inventing new ways to share relevant knowledge with blinding speed. As a direct result, markets are getting smarter—and getting smarter faster than most companies.'

Much has been made of the rise of social media and the associated networking they facilitate. But we are only just seeing the start of the impact social tools and media will have on businesses. Understandably, many businesses have taken tentative steps into the arena of blogging and wikis. Some have even started to engage on social networking sites like Facebook, Bebo or MySpace but there are two main points that we need to grasp in terms of using social media to foster engagement and the threat that an economic downturn might pose to it.

The first is to recognise that, along with search, social tools are becoming the backbone of how our customers use digital media. Human beings are inherently social creatures and will find ways to express that sociability through whatever means are available.

Digital media happen to provide better channels for this expression than anything previously invented. What *The Cluetrain Manifesto* meant by 'markets are getting smarter—and getting smarter faster than most companies' was that it is people, that is, our customers, who are getting smarter through interaction with one another in the digital space.

If this is where our customers are, then we have to be there too. In order to achieve an engaged relationship it is essential to get close to the customer. The beauty of social tools is that they are potentially available to everyone. The problem with social tools is that they require a different language to that used in many businesses. The old brand language of 'we're the greatest, look at me, follow me' has a hard time making connections in social media. It's not that the language isn't understood, it's just that it is rejected because it doesn't appear to deliver value. Marketers, and businesses in general, need to develop a light-touch if they want to use social media, a touch that offers choice and value.

The second thing that we need to recognise is that social media will become faster, cheaper and easier. As our customers use these social tools, their expectations of what experiences can be delivered will be raised. Very quickly those expectations will be applied to customer/brand interactions and relationships. If we can't deliver simplicity, fulfilment,

Barbican: Vote for engagement

London's Barbican centre, Europe's largest arts and conference venue, has generated a strong online proposition. Over the course of four years, it has raised online ticket sales from 6% to 60%. This tenfold increase has been achieved in part through the newly launched website, the design of which was informed by in-depth customer research and the observation of online booking patterns. Customers have since expressed their enthusiasm for the new online booking service.

However, the Barbican has developed a deeper experience for its online users through the inclusion of illustrative podcasts, children's games, and the extension of interactive areas.

To celebrate its 25th anniversary, a special microsite was built to focus users' attention on this important landmark in the Barbican's history. As part of this, customers were asked to vote for their favourite 25 films from Haliwell's top 100. This was not a pure statistics gathering exercise as the Barbican then went on to show the top 10 films. This was a strong demonstration of how the website was used to influence real life activity. In addition, users were also given the opportunity to suggest new content to the arts programme and submit reviews.

For the Barbican, this demonstrated how their online service went beyond improving ticket sales (although there was a boost in this area after the campaign). Customers felt that their votes counted and were able to see how they could inform the output of the venue.

speed and value on a par with the new social tools, we won't create the engaged relationships we desire.

Even the business to business world is not immune. Individuals will learn the value of social media, the value, that is, of sharing and collaborating in their private life and translate that to their business environment. These social tools can be very disruptive to businesses, but if handled well they can also provide an audience for our ideas, services and products, as well as a very serious source of competitive advantage for companies that get it right.

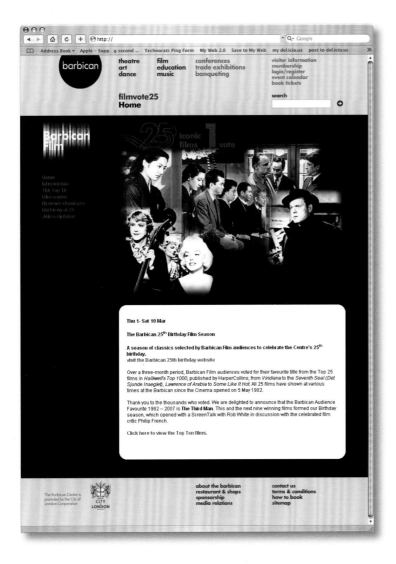

Barbican empowered its online audience to programme film screenings

www.barbican.org.uk

CIPD: Membership renewals engagement strategy

The Chartered Institute of Personnel and Development (CIPD) is the UK's leading body for Human Resource (HR) and training professionals. With a membership of over 130,000, retention and membership renewal is a key business activity for the CIPD.

In its first year of operation, early membership renewals payments increased by 277%.

The CIPD runs a sophisticated multi-channel engagement strategy, delivering member benefits, building loyalty and advocacy and encouraging repeat membership subscriptions. With the website acting as the central focus for member interactions, the organisation also provides access to exclusive content via podcasts, regular weekly newsletters, news and content feeds, peer-to-peer communities, magazines and face-to-face events and training courses.

For the past three years, the CIPD has operated a bespoke touch-strategy at the time when member renewal is required. One month prior to any requests for renewals are made, a series of 'benefits' emails are sent highlighting recent developments in services and content and encouraging members to make the most of the benefits available.

CIPD use a highly targeted and integrated approach to boost online sales

www.cipd.co.uk

Less than two months before payment is due, members are sent incentive emails encouraging early renewals with a time limited download of a report produced by CIPD's Research and Policy team. This is followed up with a series of emails and direct mail, each emphasising the different reasons that customer research has indicated motivate membership: career opportunities, peer status, access to content and services, and so on. Finally, for those members who fail to act before their membership lapses there is a reactivation campaign using email and posted letters.

In its first year of operation, early membership renewals payments online increased by 277% and online renewals prior to lapsing increased by 200%. As well as the multiple millions of pounds that were taken through the online renewals process, there were also many less obvious benefits.

CIPD employees noticed a great increase in customer satisfaction and a boost in staff morale. The benefits were felt across several departments, including the finance department which processed less posted payments. The marketing team, which handles membership growth initiatives, saw great success rates while the Research and Policy department raised its profile through the increased availability of the publication that was used as an incentive for early renewals.

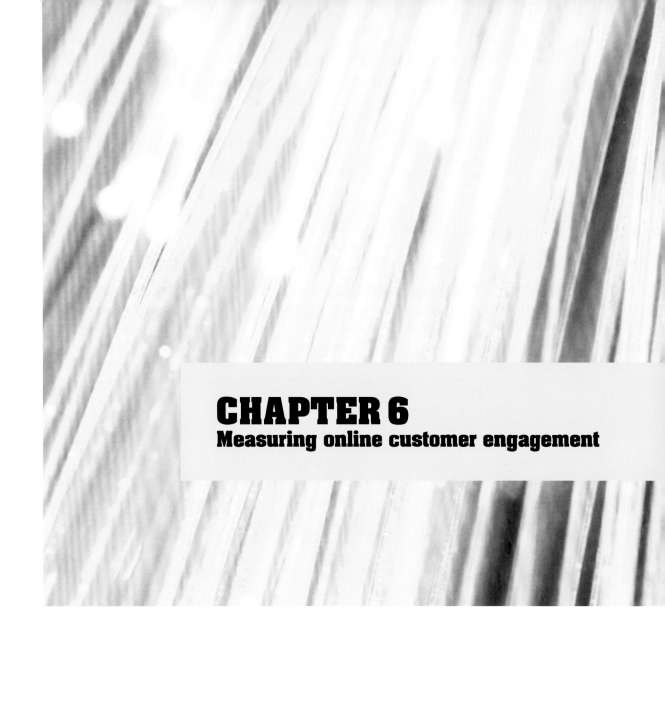

CHAPTER 6
Measuring online customer engagement

Measuring online customer engagement

The question of measurement is vitally important to any customer engagement strategy and digital channels provide opportunities to measure like no other channels do. The importance of justifying budgets and resources during times of economic uncertainty means that the role measurement plays in any digital activity is at a premium. However, often it is the sheer quantity of data gathered through digital channels that can create paralysis or mislead decision-making. Therefore, it is important to have a structured approach to gathering and analysing the data gathered through measurement activities.

Often it is the sheer quantity of data gathered through digital channels that can create paralysis or mislead decision-making.

Understanding why you're undertaking certain measurements is key to shaping a structured approach. There are three main reasons for this. Firstly, so we can assess the success or failure of our activities. Secondly, so we can understand and gain insights about our customers and how they interact with us, our services and our products in order to optimise these. And thirdly, so we can be better at predicting the impact of what we do.

Reporting is the normal expression of success or failure assessment. While it is important, often being the first activity anyone measuring digital activity is asked to perform, it is, in many ways, the least important with regards to the ongoing measurement of customer engagement.

At all times, but particularly when times are hard, we recommend focusing most of your measurement resources around the second two reasons for measuring: learning for optimisation and predicting. Taking the decision to focus on these two areas means that you can start to shape how you measure and what you measure. Key to this approach is the need to understand quantitative as well as qualitative data; an understanding of both what is happening and why it is happening.

Ideally, we combine the more traditional click-stream analysis approach (number of pages viewed, time spent on site, search, email click-throughs, etc) not just with information gained from our backend systems (number of sales or leads, service calls etc) but also with our understanding of the customer experience (surveys, user testing, face-to-face interviews etc), Avinash Kaushik, author of *Web Analytics an Hour a Day* and Analytics Evangelist for Google, has termed this approach the Trinity. A trinity based on combining behavioural understanding, business outcomes and customer experience.

Kanshik has described the benefits of this approach as: '...the Trinity mindset drives the fundamental understanding of the customer experience so that you can influence the optimal customer behaviour that will lead to win-win outcomes for your company and your customers.'[36]

It is this emphasis on win-win outcomes that is so important to effective customer engagement strategies. Doing this well, with the right emphasis on assessing your custom-

Clickstream: Click density analysis, Segmentation
Key metrics, Search, **Intent inferences**

Behaviour

To influence optimal
behaviour

Understanding explicitly
customer experience

Actionable
insights
& metrics

Experience

Outcomes

Research:
Customer satisfaction
A/B testing
Heuristic evaluation
Voice of customer

Leads: how, why
Conversion rates
Engagement
Problem resolution
Nuances of outcome

Leading to win-win
outcomes

© Occam's Razor (www.kaushik.net/avinash)

ers from all angles, provides the best means of gauging how they engage with your products, services and, ultimately, your brand.

Measuring just what was purchased, or how many times customers visited your online store—without examining their motivations, needs and satisfaction at a deeper level— could result in committing resources to the wrong activities. For example, a web team might jump to the conclusion that a website's navigation needs changing based on exit page data. In doing so, they might miss a customer's need for case studies, testimonials and UGC, elements that would help support the buying process. And why? Because they had never actually asked their customers what they wanted.

Only by looking at the customer relationship from all angles can we allocate our resources wisely and dissuade our customers from defecting. The development of your business' own specific measurements for how engaged you customers are needs to sit comfortably within this trinity approach. There is an increasing number of methodologies that have been developed to help with this. Two that are certainly worth looking at are Eric Peterson's Visitor Engagement Metric[37] and Gallup's CE11[38].

Using a combination of quantitative/qualitative testing and measuring means regular feedback on the worth of how well something is understood and used. Testing regularly and being prepared to invest in the changes needed to improve the outcomes will produce continued success. Those who neglect to remind themselves of how well their customers are actually engaging with their content, service and content regularly, will likely lose out to the competition.

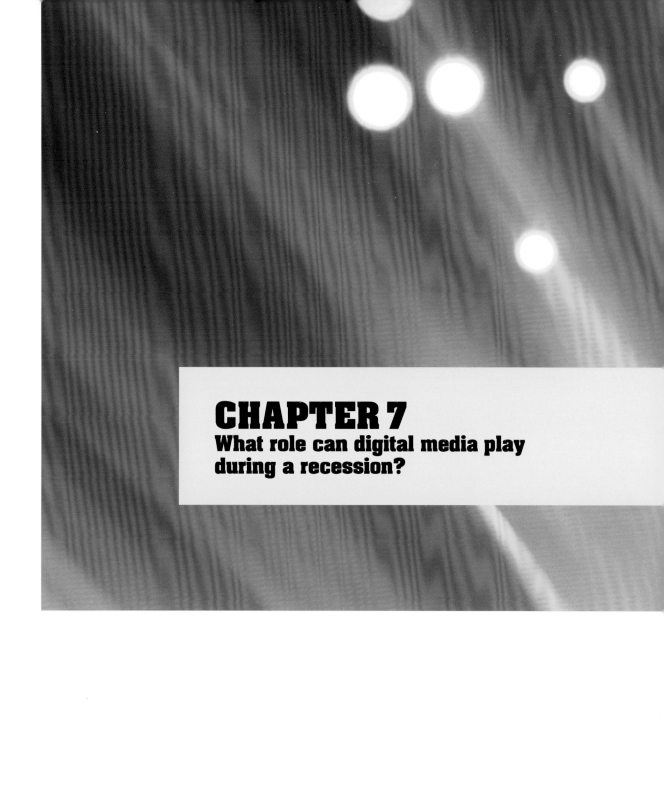

CHAPTER 7
What role can digital media play during a recession?

What role can digital media play during a recession?

We asked leading digital media experts and practitioners to give their thoughts on the implications of the economic downturn for the digital sphere.

Here, they share their professional insights on how the economic shifts have, and are likely to, effect businesses, spelling out what can be done to harness the power of digital.

If the bottom is really about to drop out of the U.S. economy, something that would surely reverberate around the world, then it is likely that advertising, marketing, and technology budgets would tighten. But unless all hell truly breaks loose, most business people will be tasked with 'doing more with less' or at least 'doing the same with less', which I think bodes well for digital.

Those marketers and business owners who have figured out how to make online audience measurement and optimisation work for them have a tremendous advantage over companies that simply 'spend money'. This is why knowing your ROI is invaluable when it is time to defend budgets. It is far easier to continue spending on marketing efforts that you can show create direct sales and drive visitor engagement, especially when you can correlate that engagement with indirect sales, consumer advocacy, and overall brand value.

Unfortunately not all business owners have developed the skills to measure their investment in digital marketing. Some companies are still looking for a silver bullet, persisting in the unnatural belief that 'measurement is easy' and that all it takes is good software. Rubbish! Web analytics is hard and requires a determined effort on the part of the organisation to integrate measurement into everything they do and then actually use the data they generate. Most companies still fail at this and therefore miss out on an incredibly valuable opportunity, one that has the ability to save budgets, jobs and entire companies.

Eric Peterson is CEO of Web Analytics Demystified and author of *Web Analytics Demystified* and *Website Measurement Hacks*

Our response to the impending recession or slowdown is not going to be the same as before. Since the last recession we have all become empowered by digital media; we have taken control of our media consumption and we have become dedicated researchers courtesy of Google. We are not the same British public we were. But what does this mean to the average business?

It means that you now have to assume that your customers and prospects are in possession of more information than you. And in harder economic times you should expect consumers to do even more research than they do today. Your customers will be researching prices, deciding if they really need a product, deciding exactly which model to buy, deciding if they want to visit your retail stores or call you on the phone. And any business which does not actively engage in this customer research activity will miss out.

So what does engaging with customer research activity mean? It means really understanding the needs of the modern digital consumer, how they research, why they come to a website, how they use it to make decisions and how they then choose to engage with the typical multi-channel business. It also means having the courage to act on this knowledge and to make changes to business as usual. It is not easy, but the economy will force companies to make these changes.

To really understand the new digital consumer and then take action across the business will require leadership at more senior levels and new skills to be developed within the business. This is the real challenge of an economic slowdown; and those organisations that couple insight, leadership and people with courage to make changes will prosper greatly.

Matthew Tod is founder and CEO of Logan Tod & Co.

There is nothing like a recession for focusing the mind of a marketer. When times are booming, less well targeted activity can still yield good results. Henry Ford was comfortable in the knowledge that only half his advertising budget was working because cars were flying off the production line with the launch of the Model T.

For contemporary marketers, proof of both results and customer understanding not only gain and maintain market lead, but justify the use and retention of budgets. The current marketplace is a tough, knowledge based environment and the digital age is providing new metrics to enable better customer segmentation to gain more predictive levels of customer behaviour.

Customer knowledge and understanding gained in boom times will continue to reap rewards when times grow lean. Cluster analysis identifies groups of customers behaving in certain ways. It can show, therefore, how certain clusters are likely to adapt their behaviour when the implications of economic change impact on their lives and consumer decisions.

Some customers will become more price sensitive, some may be more cautious, and a number will be immune to the effects of a recession. At the top end are those whose finances flourish during an economic downturn.

Lucy Conlan e-marketing consultant, cScape Customer Engagement Unit

If it doesn't play a role already, digital may be pressed into service as an alternative to more expensive traditional marketing communication programmes. This may not be the most ideal way to begin, but strategically, it's a start for those who have been urging their companies to get with it.

Ben McConnell is the co-author of the books *Citizen Marketers* and *Creating Customer Evangelists* and the blog Church of the Customer

It's really hard to make like-for-like comparison between the economic uncertainty greeting us at the outset of 2008 with downturns in the past. The fact is we have moved on. The technology stock massacre (otherwise known as the dot-com crash), is unrepeatable seven years on. The infrastructures that technology and its applications underpin are safe because none of us could now survive in a world without them.

Do without online interaction? It would be as unthinkable as the world without books and print that India's first Prime Minister, Janaharlal Nehru, tried to imagine nearly 60 years ago. We're a wired (or, more accurately, unwired) society. Cutbacks in marketing spend (the classic downturn target) won't unplug us or change our habits.

But potential cutbacks may focus attention on structural rather than 'decorating' investment. Want to spend your marketing money wisely while belt-tightening? Then think in terms of dialogue.

Concentrating spend and effort on honing and refining the 'conversations' that describe and inform our connections (how we actually talk with users through web pages, forms emails etc.), will make online interaction a more efficient, satisfactory and engaging experience than we expect— or experience—at the moment.

We go online not because we're mesmerised by fabulously convincing and persuasive creative, but because it suits us to do so. It's also massively cost-efficient for many organisations to interact online. Making it work better is the win-win option.

Online isn't broadcast. It's a one-to-one experience that with just a little investment results in more useful and satisfying (delightful, even) outcomes. Those investing in this form of direct engagement are likely to find customer retention more predictable.

Clare O'Brien is the co-founder of CDA and a senior consultant in the cScape Customer Engagement Unit

www.webwordsworking.co.uk

The merits of digital media probably just get amplified during a recession as people look for faster and more cost effective ways to communicate. The bottom line is that people are consuming more of their information online. Recent research carried out by Google has shown that Americans spend an average of 14 hours per week online and 14 hours watching TV.

So, despite any prospective recession, the mix of assets you can use online continues to grow. Wide adoption of broadband has changed the landscape to make full screen, even high definition, video content available. This combined with increasingly smart contextual marketing means that you no longer pay for a campaign and hope it hits the target audience—it *will* hit its target audience!

Steve Clayton is Chief Technology Officer of the UK Microsoft Partner Group, and author of the blog A Geek in Disguise

When the economy is booming, innovation can afford to abound and the most frivolous ideas get their share of attention and investment. From a financial perspective, the over inflation of some of those innovations, or in fact, better repackaging of existing inventions, is ridiculous. Economical uncertainties will hit Web 2.0 start-ups hard, but what about other companies investing in the digital economy? Will we see a drastic cut in web and emarketing investments?

Dot-com 1.0 was all about growing the largest client base, even if it was totally unqualified. For many, dot-com 2.0 is about gaining as much attention as possible. Except here, the concept of attention is thought of in terms of pure capitalism, that is, money and markets. Here's how the writer Michael Goldhaber defines the concept of 'attention economy': 'It is an economy in the sense that it involves allocation of what is most scarce and precious in the present period, namely the attention that can come to each of us from other human beings.'

Could Web 2.0 be something other than rich media, social media, network as a platform, Ajax, consumer generated content and all those fancy ways of reaching the end goal: 'attention '? I think so. What will remain are the concepts and the tools to help businesses, and ultimately people, become more efficient in how they allocate their attention. Blame the ongoing war in Iraq, the lead-painted toys, the housing and mortgage collapse, and volatile days on Wall Street, just like Bubble 1.0 economics, stretched Bubble 2.0 economics will be a thing of the past.

Simply put, your strategy should not get frozen during an economic ice age; it needs to adapt to its environment in order to survive. But how can you prepare?

Stéphane Hamel is an eBusiness Strategist and Web Analytics Consultant at Immeria. He is also an online instructor at The University of British Columbia

Digital marketing is useful because it can be measured so effectively. It can be used to measure offline activities too. I can see expensive 'traditional' marketing such as TV and print suffering more at the hands of the more measurable and engaging online marketing over the next few years.

When people plan their offline activities to 'land' at the online touch points you have a situation in which you can finally compare the effectiveness of many offline marketing activities which you couldn't measure before. In the old days, you developed your print ad and simply measured how many sales you got the day/week it ran. Now you can direct prospects to a specific website with more information and, at the very least, track how many who read the ad came to your website, how they reacted to your offer and compare the cost per visit to other channels.

In my opinion, social media marketing (SMM) is set to become scalable. According to eMarketer, US social networking ad-spending in 2008 will grow by 70% to $1.6 billion. A 70% growth is hardly an indicator of typical recession like activity and this is indicative of the power of digital channels. Once social networks like FaceBook figure out their business model and iron out privacy concerns this could be an exceptional way to deliver your message.

Search marketing will continue to be very important as it's one of the only methods in which every advertiser can afford to take part. Costs per click have risen but it is still by far the most measurable, cost effective and valuable way to attract prospects to your offers. With local search becoming more sophisticated and niche oriented, I can see many advertisers taking their offline ad spend to companies like Yelp which serves ads on a city by city basis.

Mobile marketing is coming. Imagine you're in a strange city and needed help to find an Italian Restaurant. How useful would it be if your mobile could direct you to the nearest one via a satellite navigation system? As an advertiser (the restaurant owner) this is a very cheap way to bring customers in. As a consumer (the hungry pasta lover) this is incredibly useful.

In summary during a recession the ability to effectively measure and determine the best ways to reach and engage customers will become more critical than ever before. Pair this with the fact that the digital channels are attractive to the consumer and the advertiser, then a recession is more likely to drive more advertising spend to the online digital channels and away from the traditional offline ones.

Steve Jackson is working for Satama and serves as the International co-chair for the Web Analytics Association

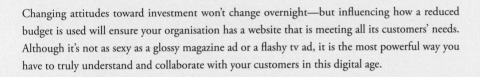 They say that when the going gets tough, the tough get going. In the case of recession, the web gets going. Having been first port of call for almost everybody when they think of initiating contact with an organisation, the website carries a heavy weight on its shoulders. It must inform, it must support offline traffic being directed its way, it must cater to online referrals and searches, and it must support loyal users who have come to expect its information at their fingertips.

However, it still surprises me that in 2008 many organisations still prioritise spending that drives all the traffic to their website, like offline marketing via TV, radio, print and mobile, but ignore the website to which they're sending people. 'We can just stick it on the website' should be banned from organisational vocabularies. And in times of economic downturn, this becomes even more critical.

With reduced spending all around and customers looking for quick, innovative ways to solve problems, the web is an obvious answer. The return on investment in small things like making your site user-friendly, and your online content easily digestable will make a big difference. If your target audiences can find what they are looking for from you the first time, whether that's by local or external search, that's a huge competitive advantage and will lead to user loyalty online—something that will bring much greater rewards when times improve and there's more money to spend.

Changing attitudes toward investment won't change overnight—but influencing how a reduced budget is used will ensure your organisation has a website that is meeting all its customers' needs. Although it's not as sexy as a glossy magazine ad or a flashy tv ad, it is the most powerful way you have to truly understand and collaborate with your customers in this digital age.

Lynda Rathbone is MD of FourSquare Media and a senior consultant in the cScape Customer Engagement Unit

www.foursquaremedia.net

The cScape/E-consultancy second Annual Online Customer Engagement Survey showed that the growing importance of digital marketing in strengthening customer relationships will be a key trend during 2008, when a compelling online experience will move from being a competitive differentiator to a prerequisite for survival.

The stormier economic waters lying in wait will force strategic minds to focus on customer retention and the different components of the digital experience which can help to increase loyalty and advocacy.

In the months ahead, consumers will be even more likely to jump ship if they do not feel in control of their environment or if they don't have the functionality and experience they can increasingly get elsewhere. From the company perspective, 2008 will be about consolidation and refinement of the best strategies and tactics for integrated and cost-effective customer engagement.

Prosperity over the coming months isn't just about having the whizziest Ajax technology or the snazziest vodcast. It's also about a joined-up proposition and experience born out of an understanding that a customer might be approaching a company from different angles and via different channels. Companies will sink or swim according to how well they deliver.

At the same time, digital marketers must reject the notion that they only need to worry about what is happening on their websites. Companies should therefore think more about going to the customer—for example on social networks or via widgets for personalised homepages—just as much as attracting them in to their own websites.

The reality is that even the most loyal customers will be spending the vast majority of their online time on other web properties. The 'atomisation' of online content and functionality, as a result of RSS feeds and open APIs, means that companies have to think about their off-site presence and engagement just as much as their own 'destination' websites.

Organisations will continue to adapt to a seismic shift in the way that information now flows more easily in all directions, rather than being controlled by organisations which broadcast their message to their customers and prospects. Word-of-mouth is now more important than ever but it should not be forgotten that customer advocacy isn't just about encouraging user-generated content.

Advocacy is a by-product of a first-rate customer experience across all channels. It is encouraging that so many digital marketers taking part in the recent cScape/E-consultancy survey see 'efficient and accessible customer services' as being an essential strategy for successful customer engagement. Getting the basics right has never been more important.

More worryingly, the 2008 survey also shows that lack of resources and experience, organisational incoherence and a lack of senior management buy-in are still barriers to better online engagement for significant numbers of companies.

When times get harder, businesses must resist the temptation to cut corners on digital marketing and make sure they strive to overcome the obstacles that stand in their way. Customers will not be as forgiving in 2008.

No area provides such granular insight in the digital media mix than search. Hence, when other media channels under perform we see shifts in client budgets towards search marketing. Not only is it a highly effective channel—mainly due to the fact that traffic and leads are already pre-qualified—but it's also highly dynamic, and performance can always be optimised to create incremental improvements in return.

It stands to reason that during a recession, as advertisers have to make cut backs and focus increasingly on low cost, high return media, that search budgets will still be justified. That said, all budgets must be squeezed during a time of recession, and search marketing will still feel the pinch. However, in terms of optimising a campaign's performance, a search marketer's work is never done anyway, so we will simply have to work harder! We may have to find more efficiency through technology rather than human intervention, and we may choose to down weight our advertising (PPC) spend in search and upweight our organic, natural search optimisation efforts.

Paid search is an auction model, and in a troubled economy there will be fewer competing bids, so search marketers can expect to pay reduced prices (or costs per click) then in more buoyant times—every cloud has a silver lining!

From a consumer perspective, a troubled economy will influence shifts in search behaviour. Firstly, the reduction in big brand and TV budgets will mean that broadcast media will be less likely to influence consumers in their search for brands and products. So search marketers will see less traffic volume around cheap brand terms, and will have to work harder at enticing searchers, as their brand awareness will be lower.

Secondly, a significant proportion of search behaviour is precipitated by scares or scaremongering. Nowhere is this more evident than in the health sector, and, consequently, with health related searches. A recession will lead to similar search trends as consumers clamour for advice on personal finance, employment and the broader economic landscape. Search marketers will need to respond sensitively by promoting rich, relevant—and ideally personalised—content to calm consumer fears.

Linus Gregoriadis is Head of Research at E-consultancy

www.e-consultancy.com

There are many strategies that get discussed when recession looms, with maximising revenue and minimising cost high on anyone's list. My preferred strategy is to use the opportunity to get as close to your customers as possible and to love them in unmistakable ways. I have many reasons for favouring this approach and not least because it is hard for anyone (we hold a budget in or outside my organisation) to argue against investing time and money in 'shoring up' client relationships. But chief among them is that I believe customers have got to want you to survive the recession. And they are more likely to do so if they like, or even better love your brand and all that it represents.

The arrival of the internet itself has been akin to a recession for many organisations with market changing dynamics being caused by dot com start ups. In my opinion many more of them are better equipped to survive and grow this time round than they were back in the 1990's. The digital media properties they have created have the ability to connect them with their customers in more meaningful ways than ever before-if they can learn how to.

Let us assume that getting the key processes in your digital property to work (i.e. be usable) is a table stake. This isn't the case everywhere but it should be given that the supply chain inefficiencies that hid usability issues in the past have almost been eradicated. This won't make anyone love you but it will stop them disliking you. If you have not yet fixed the basic usability of your property spend use whatever budget you have to do so or your survival cannot be guaranteed.

What you are left with are the small differences. The ones that shout out 'we thought about you and we made it work like this, feel like that, make your life better in this way'. These come from more creative experience design, facilitated by greater knowledge of the customer through increased research.

Recession often sees research budgets cut but I don't think this will happen to digital research budgets. Unlike the offline world the research carried out online has a direct and measurable impact on bottom line and can get you closer to your clients and allow you to create an experience they will love you for. The next step is to make sure that the experience you deliver is consistent across all your touch points on and offline. But that I fear is for another recession.

Paul Blunden is the CEO of Foviance

www.foviance.com

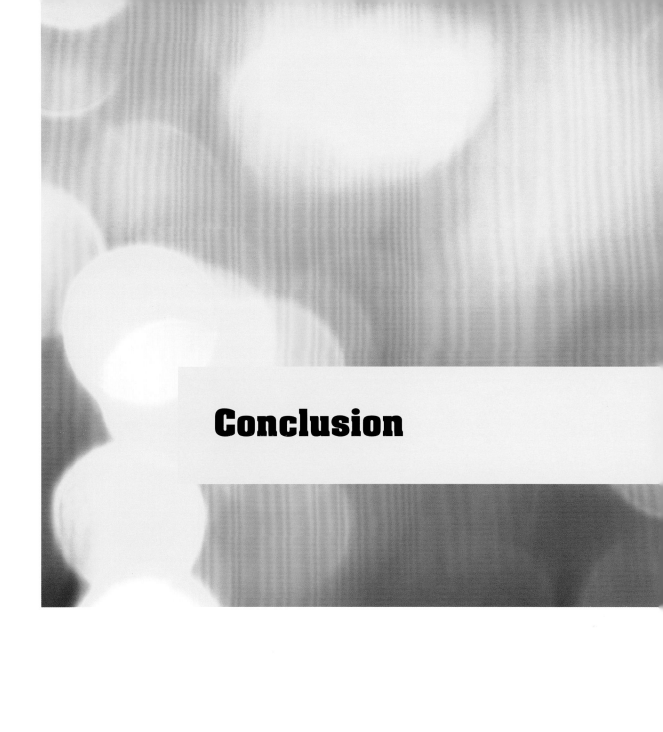

Conclusion

Conclusion

As we have argued throughout this book, online customer engagement is the best predictor of future business performance. Embracing customer engagement and adopting the use of digital media as the spine of your customer interactions, no matter what your specific market is, will give you a far better chance of not just emerging from a downturn unscathed but of emerging as a winner.

We have written this book because we want all of our clients and customers to be winners, and ultimately we want the industry in which we work and the media that so enrich our lives, to be winners too.

We hope you find this book useful over the coming period.

Martyn Perks and **Richard Sedley**

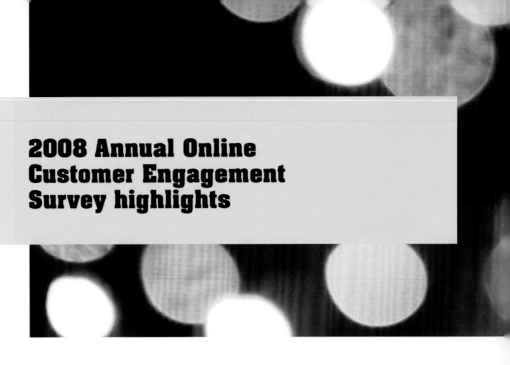

2008 Annual Online Customer Engagement Survey highlights

More than 1,000 respondents participated in the 2008 cScape/E-consultancy Annual Online Customer Engagement Survey making it the largest of its type in the world. These are just some of the highlights:

Companies are paying more attention to online customer engagement than ever before, with three-quarters (77%) of organisations saying that its importance has increased in the last 12 months. The overwhelming majority of companies (90%) now say that online customer engagement is either 'essential' or 'important' to their organisations.

Companies are using a range of methods to interact with their customers, including web-based and desktop widgets as well as participation in social networks and uploading to video-sharing websites. Around a fifth of companies (18%) say they are already using web-based widgets, while a further 39% plan to use them in the future. The idea of a widget—a third party item that can be embedded in a web page—is attractive to marketers because it can help to achieve off-site visibility and engagement.

Just under a third of organisations (32%) are planning to use social networks such as Facebook, with a further 19% already using them. Video-sharing sites are being used by

21% of companies, while a further 29% of respondents say their organisations are planning to use them in the future.

The research also found that companies are realising that they need an integrated approach which embraces all the channels used by customers. 'A consistent online and offline customer experience' is seen as 'essential' or 'very important' by 86% of organisations.

There is also evidence that more companies have actually been taking steps to deliver a more integrated experience. Since the first Annual Online Customer Engagement Report, published at the end of 2006, there has been a significant improvement in the number of organisations that are either 'very advanced' or 'quite advanced' at mapping customer experiences in order to identify different touch points.

As well as the survey findings, the second Annual Online Customer Engagement Survey Report contains comment and analysis from a range of digital marketing and web analytics experts, including Jim Sterne, Pete Mortensen, Avinash Kaushik, Dave Chaffey, Andy Beal and Richard Sedley.

You can download a copy of the report here: http://tinyurl.com/28onxs

Useful resources

Books

John A. Murphy, *Converting Customer Value: From Retention to Profit* (Wiley, 2005)

Ben McConnell, Jackie Huba, *Creating Customer Evangelists: How Loyal Customers Become a Volunteer Sales Force* (Kaplan Business, 2002)

Jim Novo, *Drilling Down: Turning Customer Data into Profits with a Spreadsheet* (Booklocker.com, 2001)

Gerald Zaltman, *How customers Think: Essential Insights into the Mind of the Market* (Harvard Business School Press, 2003)

Robert Cialdini, *Influence: The Psychology of Persuasion* (Collins, 1998)

Dave Chaffey, *Internet Marketing: Strategy, Implementation and Practice* (Financial Times/Prentice Hall, 2002)

William J. McEwen, *Married to the Brand: Why Consumers Bond with Some Brands for Life* (Gallup Press, 2006)

Seth Godin, *Meatball Sundae: Is Your Marketing out of Sync?* (Portfolio Hardcover, 2007)

B.J. Fogg, *Persuasive Technology: Using Computers to Change What We Think and Do* (Morgan Kaufmann, 2002)

Regis McKenna, *Relationship Marketing: Successful Strategies for the Age of the Customer* (Basic Books, 1993)

Christopher Locke, Rick Levine, Doc Searls, David Weinberger, *The Cluetrain Manifesto: The End of Business as Usual* (Perseus Books Group, 2001)

Chris Anderson, *The Long Tail: How Endless Choice Is Creating Unlimited Demand,* (Random House Business Books, 2006)

Frederick F. Reinhold, Thomas Teal, *The Loyalty Effect: The Hidden Force Behind Growth, Profits and Lasting Value* (Harvard Business School Press, 1996)

Paul Gillin, *The New Influencers: A Marketer's Guide to the New Social Media* (Quill Driver Books, 2007)

Bryan Eisenberg, Jeffrey Eisenberg, *Waiting for your cat to bark? Persuading Customers When They Ignore Marketing* (Thomas Nelson, 2006)

Avinash Kaushik, *Web Analytics: An Hour a Day* (Sybex, 2007)

Larry Weber, *Marketing the Social Web: How Digital Customer Communities Build Your Business* (John Wiley & Sons, 2007)

Paco Underhill, *Why We Buy: The Science Of Shopping* (Simon & Schuster, 2000)

Blogs

Agoraplace: Theo Papadakis < http://agoraplace.wordpress.com >

Captain Blackbeaks blog: Steve Jackson < http://blackbeak.conversionchronicles.com >

Church of the Customer: Ben McConnell, Jackie Huba < http://customerevangelists.typepad.com >

E-consultancy < http://www.e-consultancy.com/news-blog >

Grokdotcom < http://www.grokdotcom.com >

Groundswell: Charlene Li, Josh Bernoff < http://blogs.forrester.com/charleneli >

Internet marketing and E-marketing blog: Dave Chaffey < http://www.davechaffey.com >

Logic + Emotion: David Armano < http://darmano.typepad.com >

Loopstatic: Richard Sedley < http://www.loopstatic.com >

Marketing Productivity blog: Jim Novo < http://blog.jimnovo.com >

Marketing ROI: Ron Shevlin < http://marketingroi.wordpress.com >

nfp2: Steve Bridger < http://www.nfp2.co.uk >

Occam's Razor: Avinash Kaushik < http://www.kaushik.net >

Problogger: Darren Rowse < http://www.problogger.net >

Web Analytics Demystified: Eric T. Peterson < http://blog.webanalyticsdemystified.com/weblog >

Other resources

Wikipedia on 'Customer engagement' < http://en.wikipedia.org/wiki/Customer_engagement >

Annual Online Customer Engagement Survey (registration needed)
< http://www.cscape.com/services/Pages/CustomerEngagement.aspx >

Gallup on measuring engagement
< http://gmj.gallup.com/content/18253/What-Measuring-Customer-Engagement-Reveals.aspx >

Video: Measuring employee and customer loyalty < http://www.youtube.com/watch?v=CJGNxbMp7h8 >

Video: The new rules of engagement < http://www.youtube.com/watch?v=7kwSvoQUHyY >

Podcast: Creating Customer Value: A series with Peppers and Rogers < http://tinyurl.com/36lujc >

Endnotes

1   An adapted version of a definition put forward by Ron Shevlin, DisEngaging From ARF's Definition Of Engagement, *Marketing Whims*, 5 April 2006 < http://marketingroi.wordpress.com >

2   Nick Evans, From monologue to dialogue: changing the marketing approach, *What's new in marketing*, Issue 66, February 2008

3   Fear of recession is dominant concern among global CEOs; CEOs in emerging economies more confident than in deveoped countries, PriceWaterhouseCoopers, 22 January 2008

4   The Top 50 Up and Coming CEOs, CASS Business School, 14 September 2006

5   Egremont reveals identity of "CEO 2.0", *Top Consultant*, 21 February 2007

6   Daniel Farey-Jones, The DMA Brand Republic salary survey, *Brand Republic*, 25 July 2005

7   Sonia Soltani, Young, gifted and in the black, Building, 2006 Issue 12, and; ESAN Euroregion Skills Analysis Network < http://www.esan-project.org/content.asp?page=6 >

8   Melanie May, Weathering the economic storm, *Brand Republic*, 24 June 2003

9   Hamish McRae, Enron signals way back to robust accounting practices, *Independent*, 24 January 2002

10 Nick Evans, From monologue to dialogue: changing the marketing approach, *What's new in marketing*, Issue 66, February 2008

11 Michael Nutley, What's the big idea, *New Media Age*, 14 February 2008

12 Jennifer Whitehead, Internet ad spend growth hit by economic slowdown, *Brand Republic*, 14 January 2008

13 Jemima Kiss, Web 3.0 is all about rank and recommendation, *Guardian*, 4 February 2008

14 Adam Goodvach, Car sites need to keep up with buyers' drivers, *New Media Age*, 17 February 2008

15 Jim Novo, Marketing into a Downturn, *Marketing Productivity Blog*, 28 December 2007 < http://blog.jimnovo.com >

16 An adapted version of a definition put forward by Ron Shevlin, DisEngaging From ARF's Definition Of Engagement, *Marketing Whims*, 5 April 2006 < http://marketingroi.wordpress.com >

17 Christopher Meyer, Andre Schwager, Understanding Customer Experience, *Harvard Business Review*, 1 February 2007

18 Survey methodology note: respondents could check up to three options.

19 Frederick Reicheld, *The Loyalty Effect: the satisfaction trap, essays on the relationship between loyalty and profits*, (Bain and Company, 1996)

20 'Customer Odyssey' is a term that first came to our attention in conversation with online optimisation company, Logan Tod & Co < http://www.logantod.com >.

21 Hard sell, *Economist*, 24 January 2008

22 Ibid.

23 Nick O'Neill, No recession in sight for social web, *The Social Times*, 6 February 2008

24   Hard sell, *Economist*, 24 January 2008

25   Dave Chaffey, Right Touching - Using contextual marketing to deliver relevant messages online, 29 October 2007 < http://www.davechaffey.com >

26   *The Cluetrain Manifesto: The End of Business as Usual* (Rick Levine, Christopher Locke, Doc Searls and David Weinberger) originally started out as a set of 95 theses in 1999. It was later published in 2001.

27   Questions and Answers with Matt Shobe, *.Net magazine*, April 2007

28   Taken from William J. McEwen, *Married to the Brand: Why Consumers Bond with Some Brands for Life* (Gallup Press, 2006)

29   See J. T. Cacioppo, R. E. Pretty, *Central and Peripheral Routes of Persuasion: Application to Advertising in Advertising and Consumer Psychology* (1983)

30   B. J. Fogg, *Persuasive Technology: Using Computers to Change What We Think and Do* (Morgan Kaufmann, 2003)

31   Marketing Experiments Compendium: A year of 24 In-depth Online Research Experiments, Volume 1, Marketing Sherpa (July 2007)

32   Robert Cialdini, *Influence: The Psychology of Persuasion* (Collins 1998)

33   B.J. Fogg, *Persuasive Technology: Using Computers to Change What We Think and Do* (Morgan Kaufmann, 2002)

34   Ashley Friedlein, Publishers face the challenge of atomisation, E-consultancy, 14 December 2007 < http://www.e-consultancy.com >

35   Christopher Locke, Rick Levine, Doc Searls, David Weinberger, *The Cluetrain Manifesto: The End of Business as Usual* (Perseus Books Group, 2001)

36   Avinash Kaushik, *Web Analytics: An Hour a Day* (Sybex, 2007)

37   Eric T. Peterson, Web Analytics Demystified < http://blog.webanalyticsdemystified.com/weblog >

38   Gallup's CE11 methodology consists of 11 questions such as 'If a problem arises, I can always count on [brand] to reach a fair and satisfactory resolution.' This emphasises the emotional, qualitative side to measuring over the behavioural. It provides a very useful correction to the emphasis on behavioural data common to digital analytics. See William J. McEwen, *Married to the Brand: Why Consumers Bond with Some Brands for Life* (Gallup Press, 2006)

39   Steve is a recognized thought leader specializing with web analytics working for Satama the largest web analytics consultancy in Europe. A pioneer since 2002, he established one of the first European web analytics consultancies (Aboavista), later acquired by Satama in 2006. His clients include Nokia, Nokia Seimens Networks, Vaisala, KONE, MTV3, Vodafone, Sanoma, Vattenfall and a host of others. He is also the editor and contributing writer for the *Conversion Chronicles* website and serves as International co-chair for the Web Analytics Association. Steve has presented and keynoted web analytics topics across Europe. These include The Internet Marketing Conference (Stockholm), The Search Engine strategies (Stockholm), the IAB Finland (Helsinki), Media Plaza (Amsterdam), The eMetrics Summit (London, Munich, Stockholm), Divia (Helsinki) in addition to sitting on dozens of panels.

Index

A

AdSense network *30*
Advertising *30, 62*
Advocacy *56, 68*
AIR *48*
Ajax *42, 48, 65, 68*
Amazon *42, 52*
APIs *42*
Apple *28, 32*
Atomisation *52, 68*
   loss of control *53*
Audience diversity *21*
Audience measurement *62*
Authority *16, 22, 50*

B

Barbican *54*
BBC *48*
Bebo *21, 53*
Blunden, Paul *70*
Brand *24, 28*
   emotional attachment *43*
   emotional investment *12, 28*
   loyalty *24*
   physical investment *12*
Brochure ware *45*
Business models *66*
Business outcomes *58*

C

Cable television *14*
Chaffey, Dave *37*
Chartered Institute of Personnel and
Development *56*
Chief financial officers *14*
Cialdini, Robert *50*
Clayton, Steve *65*
Click-stream analysis *58*
Click-throughs *58*
Client relationships *70*
Cluster analysis *63*
Communication

blogs *42*
broadband *14*
broadcast *14*
   mass communication *14*
Community *21*
   peer-to-peer *56*
Conlan, Lucy *63*
Consumers *22*
   activism *16*
   behaviour *14, 38, 58, 63*
   buying decisions *36*
   decision making *58*
   decisional heuristics *50*
   demographics *38*
   evangelism *24*
   interactions *10, 12, 24, 28, 51, 54, 56, 73*
   loyalty *29*
   purchasing decision *36*
   relationships *10, 21, 24, 45, 68*
   retention *11, 24, 36*
   segmentation *38, 63*
Content *22*
   syndication *52*
Conversations *64*
Conversions *51*
cScape *29, 68*
Customer base *29*
Customer engagement *4, 10, 11, 12, 14, 15, 24, 28, 29, 31, 36, 38, 40, 42, 43, 45, 49, 50, 51, 58, 68, 73, 74*
   acquisition strategy *11*
   advocacy *68*
   conversations *53*
   conversion rates *50*
   conversions *28*
   definition of *28*
   dialogue *11, 14, 38*
   disengagement *10, 51*
   engaged relationships *28, 42*
   monologue *11, 38*
   multi-channel *56*
   strategy *36*
   successes *36*

Customer experience *58, 68*
Customer interaction *14*
Customer journeys *36*
Customer knowledge *63*
Customer lifecycle *37*
Customer Relationship Management *45*
Customer reviews *22*
Customer satisfaction *56*
Customer services *68*
    costs *29*

D

Data *58*
    analysis *58*
    qualitative *58*
    quantitative *58*
Davenport, Thomas H. *39*
Desktop widgets *74*
Digital
    channels *58*
    interaction *22*
    marketing *14, 62*
    media *10, 18, 22, 24, 42, 45*
    research budgets *70*
    technologies *14*
Distributed user experience *52*
Distribution chain *18*

E

Economy
    downturn *10, 11, 14, 28, 36, 45*
    instability *10*
    recession *10, 15, 19, 30, 46*
    slowdown *10, 14, 50, 52, 62, 63, 78*
    slump *10*
ECRM *42*
Email newsletter *38*
Employee satisfaction *29*

F

Facebook *21, 42, 48, 52, 53, 74*
Flash *48*
Flex *48*

Flickr *28*
Fogg, Dr BJ *49*
Ford, Henry *63*
Forrester *48*
Future business performance *73*

G

Gallup *43*
Google *30, 65*
Google Maps *48*
Greenpeace *32*
Gregoriadis, Linus *69*

H

Hamel, Stéphane *65*

I

iGoogle *52*
Innovation *65*
Interaction
    repeated *12*
Internet *14*
Intranets *52*

J

Jackson, Steve *66*

K

Kaushik, Avinash *58*

L

Liking *50*
Loyalty *56*

M

Market competition *22*
Marketing *14, 62*
    above the line *16*
    budgets *14*
    costs *29*
Markets
    competition *18*
    competitors *36*

markets as conversations *38*

market share *29*

profits *29*

prospects *28*

McConnell, Ben *64*

McEwen, William *43*

Measurement *58*

Media

    fragmentation *14, 19*

Mobile marketing *66*

Multi-channel *36*

    right-touching *36*

MySpace *42, 53*

N

Newspapers *19*

Niche

    interests *21*

    marketing *42*

Novo, Jim *24, 30*

O

O'Brien, Clare *64*

Online content *67, 68*

Online publishers *22*

Open APIs *68*

Opinion *22*

Optimisation and predicting *58*

P

Pay per click *30*

Perks, Martyn *4*

Personalisation *42*

    process *42*

Persuasion *50*

    as dialogue *51*

    commitment *50*

    credibility *22, 50*

    dialectics *52*

    influence *50*

    psychology *12, 28*

    role of *50*

    reciprocity *50, 51*

scarcity *50*

social proof *50*

windows *51*

Peterson, Eric *62*

Podcast *22*

PriceWaterhouseCoopers *15*

R

Radio *19*

Rathbone, Lynda *67*

Ratings *22*

Recommendations *22*

Referrals *67*

Revenue *29*

Rich Internet Applications *48*

Rich media *65*

Right-touching *37*

ROI *62*

Royal Society for the Protection of Birds *40*

RSS *42, 68*

S

Salespeople *30*

Satisfying experiences *28*

Search *58, 69*

    behaviour *69*

    marketers *69*

    marketing *66*

    optimisation *69*

    organic optimisation *53*

    rankings *33*

Second Life *42*

Sedley, Richard *4*

Silverlight *42, 48*

Social media *54, 65*

    marketing *66*

Social networks *21, 74*

Social tools *53*

Surveys *58*

T

Television *19*

The Cluetrain Manifesto *38, 53*

Tod, Matthew *63*
Touch-strategy *56*
Trust *22*
Twitter *42*

U

Unilever *16*
User-generated content *14, 22, 65, 68*
User experience *36*
User testing *58*

V

Video *42*
Video-sharing *74*
Vodcast *68*

W

Web 2.0 *52, 65*
Web analytics *62*
Websites *52*
Widgets *42, 74*
Wikis *42*
WILFing *19*

Y

YouTube *28*